Dear Bridg

Praying you will be blest as you journey through this book with Jesus, and me.

I was happy to know that you reached your 90th year!

May God add many more years of Joy, and health -

With love

Christine

June 2024

Copyright 2024

Walking with Jesus

An Autobiography

by Christine Birt

(The cover art is my own work, a painting of Moses, who I mention in this book, with one of my cows.)

Some names have been changed to protect identities.

With special thanks to

all the many wonderful people who have supported the ministry and me over the years. There are too many of you to list by name, but the Lord knows each one of you, and He, and I, will never forget all you have done.

My gratitude also goes to

Jeni Ross, Hope Walters, Robert Dougall & Nic Birt,

for helping me to publish this autobiography.

This book is dedicated to

God is Alive churches in Uganda.

All proceeds from the sale of this book will go directly to their ministry.

Walking with Jesus

By Christine Birt

Contents

The Beginning 9

Glimpses of God 21

Marriage..27

Discovering His Purpose 35

On African Soil...45

The End of a Mission The Start of a Ministry 51

The Ministry 57

Mustard Seed 73

Travelling Turmoil 89

Photos 101

A Place to call Home 121

Prison Ministry 133

Radio Outreach 153

Education and Sponsorships...157

Animal Welfare 165

Faithful Friends...179

God is Real, Religion without Him is Dead. 191

A Personal Resurrection 195

Epilogue..201

Chapter 1

The Beginning

Hello. I'm Christine, and I welcome you to read my story.

I was born the day after Christmas, in 1940. Christmas Day had always been a special occasion for my family, but from that year on, Boxing Day (26th December), my birthday, was anticipated and celebrated as well.

When I was young, Granfer (my pet name for my grandfather) bought a real Christmas tree with roots. Every year, it was replanted in the garden after Christmas, and grew at the same rate as me. Christmas was a time of indulgence and festive joy for us.

Although it was war time, and a struggle to make ends meet, I was well looked after, and always had enough. We kept chickens, and Granfer had an allotment. Also, the grownups surrendered their sweet rations to me. I was fat, and greatly loved as the only surviving child in our family.

Breaking the Curse

I am certain that my mother was cursed by a spirit of death, starting from the time my aunt, my mother, and (I think) my grandmother visited a medium (or spiritualist) to try to contact dead people. Something highly unpleasant happened during that time, which frightened them. It seemed that, from then on, everything and everyone around my mother died; my grandmother, aunt, grandfather, father, as well as mother's second husband, her little budgerigar bird, her dog, and lastly, she died.

The sin of trying to contact the dead has consequences which are visited on one's children and grandchildren. Mother had given birth to another three girls, all of whom died before I was born. The first two, named Brenda and Maureen, died at the age of 18 months, and the third daughter was still-born. (It is wonderful to know that one day we shall all meet in Heaven.)

Visiting that medium must have opened the door for the spirit of death to enter my mother's life. Even I, as a young child, was also greatly affected by it, until I was given to God at 18 months of age. This was after I succumbed to pneumonia and was at the point of dying.

There were no drugs at that time to cure pneumonia. I believe that was when Mother surrendered me to God, and for as long as I can remember, I have been aware of His Presence for the whole of my life. Thankfully Jesus dealt with that evil spirit in my life, and I was set free.

Reminder to be Grateful

I was born during the war in 1940. Throughout, and after the end of the war in 1946, life was austere, and the country was trying to recover economically. Food was rationed, there were few luxury goods, and money was scarce; we mended our clothes and made the best of what we had.

There were a lot of people in need at that time - those who had lost their loved ones, husbands, sons, and brothers. The country was left with many widows and orphans.

Every year before Christmas, Mother and I travelled by bus to Bristol city centre. There was a huge Christmas tree and an enormous box, and carols were being sung nearby. Into the box, we, along with scores of other people, would place some of our own toys which we had chosen to give as gifts for the orphans and the poor. I loved going to Bristol and giving my gifts.

The Youth Choir

I had always loved singing, and I decided to join our church's youth choir. One year, our choir was invited to sing at a Christmas service in The Lord Mayor's Chapel in Bristol. The service was recorded by the BBC (British Broadcasting Company). Later, the BBC came to record more music with the choir, in our beautiful church of St. Mary's, Shirehampton. Because the music echoed around the building, we had to sing the songs again and again, until the BBC were happy with what they had recorded. It was hard work!

A short while after this, the BBC sent payment, and we were all given quite a reasonable amount. It was the first pay that I had received in my life.

My 14th Birthday

The youth choir were all invited to my 14th birthday party. It was a very special day for me, which I shall never forget. Granfer set the table with a white linen cloth and decorated it with festive trimmings. Dad made a beautiful birthday cake, covered in icing sugar. It was a work of art, and love.

Gifts were given. I had my first pair of nylon stockings, some perfume, talcum powder, bath salts – all kinds of feminine gifts. Our beloved curate, Geoffrey Griffiths, gave me a book that showed every type of dog breed - I was the proud owner of one little terrier dog!

Then we sang beautiful carols in four-part harmony. It was Heaven to me.

Dad

My dad was the best father in the world, and he and I loved each other very much. After the war, Dad worked as a fitter at Avonmouth Docks in Bristol. He was also the Transport and General Workers Union elected representative.

His work kept him busy from 7am till 4pm daily, and occasionally up until 6pm. But, on Sundays, he always finished at 3pm, and brought home two boxes of chocolates: one for my mother, and one for me. My dad was kind, loving, and never lost his temper. He was well respected by everyone.

When I was 11 years old, I had to take an exam which decided whether I would go to Grammar School or Secondary School. My dad promised me that if I passed for Grammar School, he would buy me a bicycle.

I passed the exam, but Dad told me I had to wait patiently until he had saved up enough money for the bicycle. My father was a man of his word, and after some months he bought me a big, old, black, second-hand, 'sit up and beg' Hercules bicycle. It was wonderful!

When I was learning to ride, Dad ran after me, holding the saddle to steady me. He was good - he ran hard, and I never fell off.

Once I was able to ride properly, we would go out for long rides on our bicycles together. He taught me the Highway Code, how to position myself on the road, and even how to service my bicycle… My good dad, how I loved him.

Dad somehow managed to save up every year for a family holiday, in a caravan by the sea at Bournemouth. There we relaxed together and had the chance to swim in the sea every day, which I took full advantage of.

I am so thankful I grew up with such a close, loving family.

Granfer (my grandfather)

"What's up old soldier, no beer today? What a pity, what a pity, what a pity!" Our small budgerigar, Peter, sang this song over and over. Granfer had taught it to him.

Granfer had been a professional cavalry soldier and a Sergeant Major in the Royal Horse Artillery. He was upright in stature, but walked with a slight limp because of a wound sustained in the First World War. His horse was shot from under him, and it fell, trapping his leg under all that weight. It troubled him for the rest of his life.

Every Christmas, Granfer received a special 'thank you' letter from an officer in his regiment. It was rumoured that the officer was wounded in no-man's land, and that Granfer went out, and carried him back to safety, all under enemy fire. I never doubted it to be true, because it was exactly the type of thing a man like him would do.

Granfer ruled his house with a rod of iron, in true Victorian style. Whatever he demanded was immediately fulfilled. But he always showed true tenderness toward my mother and me.

His greatest love was his flower garden. It was a burst of colour, beauty, and delicious perfumes. He designed it with regimental precision, and along the front part he wrote a different motto in flowers every year. Once, he planted a floral clock, along with the proverb 'Time and Tide Wait for No Man.' It was greatly admired. People came from miles to see it.

One day, when I was about three or four years old, I was 'helping' him plant out his seedlings for the coming year. Whatever it was that he was busy planting with such care, I was following him, equally busy, pulling them all out!

When he saw what I was doing, he shouted to my mother, "Vi! Come and take this child!"

Granfer never raised his voice at me, and I know he loved me deeply.

A Shared Passion

Granfer was the proud owner of a large mahogany cabinet, which stood about the height of a table. The lid lifted to reveal a gramophone, and it had a deck which played '78' records. You lifted the arm, which had a needle attached, and placed the needle carefully at the outer edge of the revolving record, and music came out. Oh, how I loved that device!

Because I was quite a careful child, Granfer decided that I was allowed to use it. I sat over that gramophone for hours, listening to Danny Boy, The Rose of Tralee, and Sparky's Magic Piano. (How I wished I could play a piano like that… Yet, one day I was given a piano, and learned to play - but not like Sparky!)

I listened to Sandy Macpherson sing about the poor little goldfish goin' round and round, with no father or mother, and a song about the disgrace of someone going to a funeral wearing brown boots, and a whole host of other songs.

Granfer on Sunday

When I was about 15, I asked Granfer to come to Church with me for Evensong. To my amazement, he came. He said he was not able to hear the preaching, because he was a little deaf, but they sang his favourite hymn which was, 'The day thou gavest Lord is ended, the darkness falls at thy behest.' It was quite a surprise to me that Granfer knew any hymns. I had never known him to set foot inside a church!

He usually went into the village on Sundays, and drank with his mates at the Life Boat pub. He came home at 2 o'clock to eat his Sunday lunch, and then go to sleep.

One Sunday, he was later than ever, so I said to my mother, "Let's go, and bring him home."

We put on our coats and went for him. He was utterly astounded to see us walk into the pub, and he came home with us as quiet as a lamb. In those days, it was not normal for women to go to pubs.

Illness Strikes

Granfer was a great smoker. Cigarettes became expensive, so he decided that he would plant the whole of the back garden with tobacco plants. (I think this may have been illegal.) People were asking about the lovely green plants with the good smell that he was growing. He harvested his tobacco and hung the big leaves on string lines in the kitchen to dry. After drying, he smoked it all.

He was soon to be diagnosed with lung cancer. What made things worse for me personally was that, from the time he was diagnosed, I was not allowed to go to hospital to see him. My mother feared that I might tell him that he was going to die. I could never hide anything. If he had asked, I would have told him the truth.

God's Mercy

Granfer suffered terribly. One day, my mother and her sister Aunt Dorrie came home after visiting him, and they sat in chairs opposite each other in an awful silence. I knew the situation was really bad.

That weekend would be the first Easter Sunday that I would take Communion since I had been confirmed. So, when it was time to take Communion, I made an extremely specific and intentional prayer, asking Jesus to please take Granfer, because the suffering was unbearable.

When I reached home, all the curtains in the house were drawn. This used to be the custom whenever anyone died in those days. When I went in, I found out that Granfer had died. The nurse had said that it was not necessary to give him his last morphine injection. I was shocked. God had answered my prayer immediately. The suffering was over.

I believe the prayer was good because I handed him over to Jesus, and I trust Jesus. I have no idea where Granfer is now.

After his death, we left that house to move into a smaller home. The lady who went to live in the old house said that one day Mr Lewis (Granfer) had brushed past her going down the stairs, and he was in a very bad temper. ***Something*** had been left behind!

Chapter 2

Glimpses of God

When I was working in a library in the UK, in the 1970s, I found myself very hungry for God. I remember that I read a book at that time called 'Hungry for God'. I wanted desperately to know the real God. Where could I find Him? I read all kinds of books about the devil, and I knew that he was there, and had power. I enjoyed reading about death. I believed in God, and in Jesus. I attended Church regularly. I loved Church I wanted to be there all the time. I felt the Presence of God there, but when I came out, I left Him inside.

I knew I should show love to others, but I didn't always find it an easy task. There was a woman, Debby, that I used to work with, who was rather unpleasant. Nobody liked her, and I found that I was no different. Knowing what my attitude should have been towards her, I prayed about it.

I admitted to God, "I am supposed to be a Christian, yet I do not like this woman."

An impression came into my mind that I should buy Debby a little cake. You know, a small cupcake. So, I bought one and gave it to her. She ate it and was completely changed from that moment. She became my friend, and everyone began to like her.

About this time there was a chaplain's Assistant at the RAF Base (where I lived) who brought books for me to read. They were about the

Holy Spirit, gifts of the Holy Spirit, miraculous healing, revivals all over the world, and about the devil. I realised I had sinned by allowing the devil to come into my life through the books I read, and I repented.

One day I told the chaplain, "I have never seen God heal anybody."

Maisie said, "Christine, I want you to come with me to a healing meeting in Bedford then you will see."

We went. I was amazed to see a rather ordinary looking Pastor pray for a line of people.

As he was praying for one lady using a walking frame, she looked up at him, and said, "Pastor, the pain has gone."

He stopped and taught her to walk. She began walking, then running around the church. It was the beginning for me of seeing the power of God at work in the Church. Since then, I have seen Him open deaf ears and blind eyes, and heal the lame, and cause legs to grow.

One day a man came to me in the library and showed me a piece in a book which said, "The last enemy that will be overcome is death."

He said, "This is true, isn't it?"

I shot up an arrow prayer to God, "Are you talking to me?"

As I was praying, a librarian answered a phone.

She looked me in the eyes, and said, "Yes, Christine. Right."

I was amazed that God could speak to me so directly as soon as I had asked. I called Maisie, and she came to my home and led me to Christ that night. From that moment I was changed. Completely changed. That night, as I went to bed, I was not afraid to look into the mirror. A demon of death had been following me for most of my life and was always looking back at me from every mirror, but *this* night there was only Christine looking backout of the glass. I had finally met with God. I was changed. My fears had gone. No longer was there any fear of the dark, of flying, of snakes. I was highly aware of Jesus with me. Boldness came. I wanted to let the whole world know that Jesus Christ is alive. He is always there. Closer than the air we breathe.

A great peace had come upon me, and I was exhausted. I slept that night without dreams; a deep, healing, peaceful sleep. Since then, I have found that I rarely have any dreams. I think if I dream these days God might be revealing something to me. I have always slept well from that time onwards.

After this, I met every week with a house group who practised the gifts of the Holy Spirit. We spoke in tongues, interpreted tongues, prophesied, and healed the sick. I was so happy.

One day at work, Debby told me that she was suffering with gout, a painful ailment, in her feet. I told her I was going for a prayer meeting that night. Would she like us to pray for her?

She exclaimed, "Oh yes! I would like that."

I said that it would be at 8 o'clock that night. She was at home that evening, and when she happened to look over at the clock, it was exactly 8pm. She realised all the pain had left her feet. She was healed!

I was so happy at the home group and with all that was happening, that was until one day I had a strong desire to meet with God through the Holy Spirit. At a prayer meeting I was urged to speak out message in tongues. But. I was reluctant, thinking **Perhaps this is not God,** and, **What will the others think of me**. Some minutes passed as we all waited for God to speak to us. I grew hotter, and hotter, and then another person spoke out the very same message in tongues. I was so ashamed that I had not obeyed the prompting of the Holy Spirit. That week during my prayers, I promised God that if He urged me to speak in tongues again, I would speak.

I thought that He would never use me again, but then at the very next weekly prayer meeting the urge to speak in tongues came. Straight away I spoke it out, before any other thought could enter my head. Immediately another person in the group interpreted the tongues, which was a message of praise, and worship.

As we were leaving several people came and encouraged me, saying it was a beautiful tongue that God had given me. It was a huge learning curve. What a loving, forgiving, teaching, Holy, and tender-hearted Father we have.

Chapter 3

Marriage

After school I began to work in the physics dept. of University of Bristol as a microscopist, and a balloon maker (balloons 300 feet long, to rise into the ionosphere carrying stacks of photographic plates).

I met a young man working in the photography department. He was shooing a small kitten down the stairs, and out of the building. I thought he was a horrid man treating the kitten so badly. Yet, that was the man I married six years later.

He pursued me relentlessly and travelled home with me every day. I had prayed about marriage, and had asked God for a handsome, tall, fair-haired man. I wanted a Christian who never smoked or drank alcohol.

Alan fulfilled the necessary qualifications, and in due time we married in St Mary Redcliff Church in Bristol, one of the most beautiful Anglican churches in Britain. We made our vows to love and be faithful to each other.

The priest tied us together with his stole (a vestment like a scarf), saying, "Those whom God has joined together, let no man put asunder."

Travelling and Family Life

My husband was sent away almost immediately, for basic training as an education officer in the Royal Air Force. He had already trained as a teacher. Our life in the RAF began with a posting to Kinloss, in the north of Scotland.

After two years, our first son was born in Elgin cottage hospital, and we called him Timothy Edward (after his paternal grandfather). After his birth, I was finally fully accepted into what was an extremely tight-knit, Scottish - Highland community. I had borne their son, and as a boy, he was called a loony.

We were then posted to RAF Hereford, where we were given married quarters to live in. 19 months after Timothy's birth, Nicholas Charles (after his maternal grandfather) Birt arrived in Hereford hospital, and our family was complete. God had granted my prayer request for two sons, either twins or close together.

Our life together was good, and I was happy and content with my husband and children. We were strong Christians, never missing church. We brought the boys up in the Anglican tradition, and they sang as choirboys. *HOWEVER,* God was pursuing me, and gave me a deep, persistent hunger to find Him, the true living God.

Then it happened!

Encounters that Changed Everything

The Chaplain's Assistant at RAF Cosford was giving me books to read on the work, and the gifts, of the Holy Spirit. Then she took me to a healing service, and I saw a woman walk into church on crutches.

When the pastor had prayed for her, she looked at him and exclaimed, "Pastor! The pain has gone!"

She started to walk, and dance, and finally run around the church. I was so happy!

I recall when I was in Jerusalem, and visited the tomb of Jesus, I sensed the words, 'Why are you seeking the living among the dead?' It was special moments like this that fed the hunger in me for more of God.

Another time, I was praying in a chapel on an RAF base at Cosford. On the altar was a cross which had an image of Jesus carved into it. He was not hanging on the cross in pain. He was standing in the cross with His arms outstretched, wearing a crown, and kingly robes. I sensed His Presence there. He held out His hands to me, wanting me to look into the horrible wound in one of His wrists. I was reluctant, but when I looked, I saw a name was written in the wound. It was Christine. One Psalm says, 'See I have tattooed your name on the palms of my hands.' (Isaiah 49:16)

It was around that time that I surrendered fully to Christ and experienced His Presence. Soon after, I felt Jesus touch me on the head when I was praying in my bedroom, and I was filled with warmth from the top of my head to the tip of my toes. Before long, I also began to speak in tongues... I was moving in the power and gifts of the Holy Spirit... I had come ALIVE!

It was a dramatic change, and my husband was not happy.

One evening, I sat with him and told him what had happened to me. I began by saying that this God, whom we had been worshipping all our lives, was real. When I finished talking to him, I left him with a question, which if he had answered yes to, he would have been saved.

He said, "I see that something has happened to you, and your face is shining. I will never stop you, but I will never be involved with it."

At that moment a shutter came between us. It was too much for him. Although we continued to live together for a while, he wanted me to divorce him, which God would not allow. So, after two years of separation, he divorced me. He went on to marry another woman, who already had two sons called Timothy and Nicholas.

To this day, I remain unmarried. I am separated now unto God. ALL things work together for good to those who love God, and are called according to His purposes. (Romans 8:28)

He Heals the Broken Hearted

I loved going to healing meetings. In one meeting, the evangelist happened to glance at me for less than a second, but when his eyes met mine, I saw Jesus' eyes accepting me.

Another time, I went to a camp meeting where we stayed in tents, and held our meetings in a big tent. (This was at Hollybush, some of you know this place). The speaker gave the invitation for people to accept Jesus as their Lord and Saviour. I had to go forward, although I was saved.

A counsellor met me there and was quite disappointed to find that I was already a believer, because she really wanted to lead someone to the Lord. I told her my husband had left me, and she counselled me very well, but nothing happened.

I was kneeling, and then suddenly I realised I could not stand. My legs seemed to have grown roots into the ground. I looked up at the microphone, and it changed into the Cross of Jesus. He was hanging there in great pain. He looked at me. Blood was flowing out of him.

I forgot about all the other people, and I wept, and wept, and wept. I could only see Jesus. When at last the crying stopped, a great peace came into my heart. My broken heart was healed.

Another Phase of Life Begins

The years passed, and my children grew up and left to make their own way in the world. I accepted that my role as a homemaker and carer for the boys was now over. A new phase in their lives was beginning and I was happy for them.

I was content to live with Christ alone, but at the same time, I couldn't help wondering, what was I supposed to do with my time? What was my role in life now, and what did the Lord expect of me? How could I be more useful for his Kingdom? Should I just stay where I was, continuing to be a faithful attendee, serving at church where I could, in a quiet, unseen way? These questions plagued me for some time before any direction came.

Chapter 4

Discovering His Purpose

"There is plenty of work for young people, but nothing for older people like me!"

At 49 years of age, there still was a deep longing in my heart. It was crying out to do more for God, and God was listening. I woke up one night, hearing someone speaking in my room. As I came to, I realised I was speaking to myself.

I cried out again and again, "What shall I do?"

Then, I heard an audible voice say, "Lift up your hands."

As I lifted my hands and began to praise God, I stopped agonising over what to do. In and from that moment, I was surrendering to Him instead.

Very soon after, I found out about Crossroads, a 4-month long discipleship course, run by Youth With A Mission (YWAM), at King's Lodge in Nuneaton. It was for older people who had reached a crossroad in their lives. I felt strangely drawn to apply, but first I went to Birmingham to talk with the Director of YWAM there. He prayed with me, and was given the scripture, 'You have not chosen Me, but I have chosen you, and I have appointed you, that you might go, and bear fruit, and keep on bearing, and that your fruit may be lasting' (John 15:16).

A Step of Faith

Having found the assurance I needed, I decided to apply. After a short while, the YWAM leaders (who had been praying regarding my application) heard from God that it was right for me to be there, and I was accepted.

It was then that I discovered the course, including an outreach at the end, would cost £1,500. This was very expensive in 1990. I looked at my small savings... £50!

Suddenly, God spoke clearly to me, "Give it away!" (I had learned to hear the voice of the Holy Spirit, as I prayed every day).

Okay! I withdrew the money, leaving £5 to keep the account open. Looking around the bank, I noticed an appeal was being made for earthquake victims. I gave the money towards that appeal, and immediately felt relieved. I always feel relieved when I obey His voice. It did not matter where the money went, just as long as I gave it away.

However, walking out of the bank, I said to myself, *Now what have you done?*

But, before long, people I knew from all over the country began to send me money, until I had the complete £1,500! Another provisional miracle, orchestrated by my wonderful, faithful Saviour.

Back to School

The time came, and I locked my small flat and set off for YWAM. But, I was not looking forward to sitting in a classroom for all those months.

Why was I doing this? I was not a youth.

However, Jesus had been my Lord and Saviour since 1975, and I knew Him. He taught me much as I read and re-read the Bible. I had also been to conferences (such as the American John Wimber for Pastor's - Signs, and Wonders, Healing, and Deliverance) where, not only did we hear the Word, but we witnessed miracles with our own eyes.

Before that, I was part of a Women's Intercessory Prayer Group, called Lydia. We prayed for our nation and had wonderful annual conferences where we learned to listen, pray, and know our God.

The day after I arrived at King's Lodge, I discovered why I was there. We were told our outreach was going to take some of us to Egypt, some to Kenya, and some to Uganda.

That was it! My heart leapt with joy. God was taking me to Uganda!

King's Lodge Nuneaton YWAM 1990

The YWAM teaching was good, as were the practical sessions. After every session, the Holy Spirit was invited to minister, and some interesting manifestations occurred. But, despite all this, I was never happy sitting day after day in the classroom. Every evening I went for a walk to blow the cobwebs away with Brenda, the oldest student on the course.

Brenda was from Scotland and was over 70 years old when we met. She had a real love for Jesus. One evening, at dusk, Brenda injured herself falling into a deep ditch. I helped her get back to base, and she asked me to bathe and check her wound. It looked bad, so we prayed. Afterwards, the injury was treated, and thankfully she recovered well. Somehow, that incident bonded us together. We soon found we had common interests and became really good friends.

Hands-On Healing

A minister from the USA, called Dave Duell, came to help the students operate in the healing ministry. He was great fun. He had been a cowboy and had begun his healing ministry by practising on his sick cows!

He started by ministering to the students and praying for each one. When my turn came, Dave scrutinised me from head to toe with X-ray eyes, pointing out various parts of the body where past injuries had left various aches, and pains. Then he blew on me, and I felt myself twirling away in a small whirlwind. When it was over, I found myself healed completely.

A YWAM staff member had come back from an outreach in Africa with a strange sickness, which kept her bound in a wheelchair. After Dave prayed, she was healed, and left her wheelchair as a testimony.

I partnered with Brenda, my elderly friend from Scotland, to pray for each other under Dave's watchful eye. When I sat with my back up against the chair, my legs stretched out in front of me, I saw that one of my legs was a little shorter than the other.

Thinking nothing of it, I closed my eyes and Brenda prayed. As she did so, I felt *someone* catch hold of my big toe and give it a yank! When I opened my eyes, both legs were the same length!

I asked Brenda, "Did you catch hold of my toe?"

"No, it wasn't me." she replied.

Well, well! The Great Physician was healing me!

For a few days after, I found myself walking with a slight limp. I had unwittingly been used to walking with one leg shorter than the other for so long, some readjustments had to be made.

More Miracles

Some weeks into the course, the leaders told the students that because of the outreach taking us to Africa, a further £600 would be needed. Yet another substantial sum back in 1990! As I wondered how I would find the money, I had a thought to go into Nuneaton and inquire in the shops to see if any needed an assistant in the evenings and on Saturdays. One shop-owner was interested and asked me to come back for an interview the following evening.

I agreed, but there was a problem - I was feeling quite feverish. As a soldier about to go on active service, I had had several vaccination jabs for a host of diseases that are unheard of in the UK, a necessary precaution for those wishing to travel to Africa. The fever must have been a side effect.

As I walked back in the cold and dampness of the coming spring, I prayed, "Lord, I went out looking for a solution to my problem, without consulting You first. I am sorry. If it is not Your will that I take this job, please provide another way."

I felt the peace of the Lord come at that moment.

A woman had tried to phone me at the Base while I was out, and had left her number for me (there were no mobile phones yet). So, I called the lady back to ask what she wanted.

She explained, "I feel God is telling me to give you some money. I have just put £600 into your bank account."

Wow! Jesus is alive.

Evangelism

At last, we came to the time of outreach on the course. My spirit began to rise within me. There was pavement evangelism ministry, where dramas were performed, and the Gospel preached on the streets of Nuneaton. On the whole, the British public was embarrassed and tried to avoid both the performances and the preaching. The Great British Reserve!

A team of us went into an old people's home, and I saw an old woman crippled up with arthritis. When I asked if I might pray with her, the lady was glad, and agreed.

Laying hands on her, I was led to ask, "Is there anyone that you have not forgiven?"

The lady was surprised and said, "Yes."

I prayed and broke the power of un-forgiveness, and the lady was able to pray and forgive that person.

Then she looked at me, astonished, and said, "The pain is gone!"

Even her gnarled hands began to open up!

If we refuse to forgive, we harm ourselves. Bitterness turns inward, and sickness follows. It may even end in death.

Chapter 5

On African Soil

Stepping off the aircraft onto Kenyan soil, in the early morning coolness, breathing the pure air was sweet. Tall palm trees were gently fluttering in the breeze. We had arrived. It was magical.

Nairobi was another world. The team stayed in a house together and evangelised in one of the most notorious slums in Africa, and in a richer neighbourhood.

The slum was a shanty town, its dwellings a mixture of mud, iron sheets, timbers, and cardboard boxes, and the aroma that filled the air was a mixture of cooking and sewage. The people in the slums loved the Gospel and wanted to receive salvation. Many were healed. It was amazing.

In the richer area, the team went from door to door. The houses were enormous, and had huge compounds with high walls, guards, and dogs. In fact, it was impossible to gain entry. My team failed to reach even one owner. How hard it is, for a rich man to enter the Kingdom of God! (Matthew 19:23)

Adventures in Eldoret

The team moved on from Nairobi to Eldoret, for more evangelism. The accommodation was a sort of hotel, which catered for the local prostitutes at night. I shared a room with two of the sisters on the team. They prayed, cleansing the room with the Blood of Jesus, and anointing their beds with oil before they climbed in to sleep. Footsteps were heard throughout the night, and on one occasion a woman was heard screaming.

In the bright light of another warm morning, the night seemed like it had just been a dream. There was tea to drink, bread, and jam, and hard-boiled eggs. It was so normal. Waiters in white coats went to enormous trouble to put the team at ease.

The days were spent in a village, going from door to door. The houses were all made of mud, some with iron sheet roofs, and others were grass thatched. The team was warmly welcomed, and we prayed with lots of people.

The finale came on the last night, when the team performed small dramas and preached the Gospel. An appeal was made, and the whole village came forward to receive Jesus as their Lord and Saviour. As we looked up into the beautiful night sky, there was a crescent moon and an accompanying small star. It was the manifestation of a vision we had when we were praying for the outreach. The Holy Spirit fire had fallen, and we rejoiced.

When my son, Nic, was 18 years old, he had spent 10 months with Africa Inland Mission, at a school a few miles down the Rift Valley. The Rift Valley is quite near to Eldoret, and one day while we were there, I was given permission to go and visit the school.

Another member of the YWAM team, David Ardron, accompanied me, and we were introduced to the joys of travelling by public transport. We were rammed in together, travelling at dangerously high speeds in vehicles that would have been condemned to the scrap heap in the UK.

The view, however, made up for the unpleasant travelling experience. It was absolutely breathtaking going down to the Rift Valley, where the school was located.

Uganda

The next day, we boarded the bus for Uganda. The journey was horrendous. The road had the appearance of having been bombed, because it simply had not been repaired in years, if ever. The potholes were deep and enormously wide, and the driver skirted around the rims - they called it wheel balancing. The drive took most of the morning.

Crossing at the hottest part of the day, we arrived at the town Malaba. It was like an oven. The border officials took hours. The toilets stank. Water was scarce. I wondered whether I would ever be cool again.

At last we made it over the roughest part of the journey, and we found ourselves travelling on a much more reasonable road to the Jinja YWAM base. Once we got there, the arrival of the 37 travel-weary YWAMers caused great excitement. The rooms were filled with triple bunkbeds. I was assigned a top bunk. A card and a small gift of ground nuts welcomed me.

'It is a *pressure* to have you,' the card declared.

I thought, *Surely it must be so.*

Chapter 6

The End of a Mission
The Start of a Ministry

When I decided to come to Uganda with YWAM, I had a strong impression that God was calling me there and that it would be long-term. In fact, I told my leaders in YWAM this, and said I would be taking extra things with me in case I was asked to stay. They agreed, as they also believed that I was hearing from God.

After the outreach in Uganda came to an end, Okumu, a young pastor who had arranged the outreach in the village, invited me to stay. My leaders agreed.

The other team members went back to Nuneaton, and I remained in Uganda with YWAM for a while. I began to prepare to minister in the village churches with Okumu and his fellow minister, Andrew Mutengu.

When I finally left YWAM, I was under the umbrella of Deliverance Church. Every weekend I would report to the Pastor in Jinja and stay overnight in a boys quarter. After that, Okumu, Andrew and I came under the umbrella of Pastor Robert Kayanja, at the Miracle Centre in Kampala.

Settling In

It was 1990. I had been in Uganda for over half a year and was living with the culture officer,

Teddy, in Kamuli. She gave me a room that had been plastered with cement, and had one window with wooden shutters, and iron bars for security. Okumu and Andrew were also living in her boys quarters.

Living with a Ugandan family meant that life was very difficult. Teddy bought me a mattress, and I slept on the floor with a mosquito net over me. I had the one suitcase that I came with. I was unable to manage the communal bathroom (a cement room with a plug hole in the corner), so I bathed in my room with a basin of water. The others laughed and called it dry cleaning.

There was still rebel activity at that time. One morning, before dawn, there was a loud knocking on our door.

I heard Teddy open it and say, "Oh, you are most welcome!"

Then soldiers came into the house and searched it, looking for rebels. They were greatly astonished to find a white woman, sleeping on the floor with one suitcase by her side. They asked whether I had any photographs, but I didn't. Eventually they went away, but not before they cut open our drum to see if there were any weapons inside.

These were regular events in the life of the locals, but it was all an educational and eye-opening experience for me. I saw real poverty at that time.

Later, when I rented my own premises, Okumu lived in my small house in the boys quarters. He was married to Sarah at the time. Sarah came back to live in the house with him when they were first married. Andrew also had a quarter with me. The two men came with their younger brothers. Andrew married Sarah's sister, and now they have grown up children. The younger brothers were educated in the UK. Living Water Ministries took one, who is now a chemist and is married.

Both my sons married when I was in Uganda, and I felt tremendously sad that I was not able to attend either of their weddings.

Living Waters helped me a great deal. They even sold my small flat in the UK, and sorted everything out for me while I was in Uganda.

Seeing Christmas with Different Eyes

Foolishly, after 7 months, I decided to return to the UK for Christmas. I went into a supermarket and saw people loading trolleys with food and alcohol. So overwhelmed was I by the amount of food in the store, that I was unable to decide which of the many cereals I should buy and came out with nothing!

At the entrance, some people had collection boxes for a charity, and I saw people from the store coming out and putting their small change into the boxes, after spending hundreds of pounds to indulge in Christmas.

        I felt nauseated. Uganda was now in my blood. I had left there only to visit my small family, and I knew I had to go back.

Chapter 7

The Ministry

3 years after leaving YWAM, we would move from where we were based in Kamuli, to go to Mbale. Living Water Ministries, UK, were supporting me in intercessory prayer, and a group of them occasionally came to Uganda.

They asked me to help them begin their ministry in Mbale. God had spoken to them to come to Mbale. Of course, I was not able to manage this, but Okumu worked it all out practically.

We came to Mbale, and Okumu and Andrew began the work of God.

The Battle to Stay

Several times I felt that I could not go on in Uganda. A great number of things annoyed me. Once, I ran away, and went into the village where we began our ministry together. Okumu found me.

"I'm fed up, and I am going back!" I told him.

He asked me, "Has God told you to go back?"

I knew he was right, and in the end, I found I just could not go back… God had brought me for His purposes. (I came to Uganda for six weeks, and have remained for 33 years!)

Busamaga

Some years after I came to live in Uganda, I moved to a new house. I left my first one because the landlord raised the rent, and so I moved to Busamaga. It was on the edge of Mbale town, going into the village, and was a trading centre.

I found a cheaper place, with a large compound for my animals. We had some cows and a few donkeys, as well as our dogs. The house had plenty of room, and even a fairly well-appointed boys quarters that could be rented out. The new landlord was all smiles and charm. A few days before Christmas, we moved lock, stock, and barrel, as the saying goes.

Muzungu

(Meaning a Rich or a White Person - both are considered the same here in Uganda!)

A day or so after I arrived in Busamaga, one of my dogs brought a dead turkey into the kitchen. I was aghast. I discovered that some turkeys had come through a small gap into the compound to eat my ducks' food, and the dogs had been having a great time chasing them. The turkeys were not quite fully grown, and all had huge growths over their faces, one of the horrible signs of fowl pox.

"What should I do?" I asked the neighbours.

No one knew who owned the turkeys. When I returned to the kitchen, I found the turkey had resurrected, and was standing. I picked it up and took it to the LC1 (the local government chief). He was not there, so I left the bird with his wife, briefly explaining that I could not find the owner.

The next day, there was battering on the gate by an angry man, demanding that I pay for his turkey.

I thought, *these villagers think that there is a white woman here, who they are going to fleece for every shilling possible!* So, I simply told them the turkey had been trespassing.

Nightclub Nightmare Neighbour

The neighbours played loud disco music, and within the nearby market area were two cinemas playing their entertainment loud enough for us to hear well. The neighbouring hairdressers, and boys selling music, were all also playing tunes loudly. I was surrounded by noise. Everyone playing different music, and all at the highest possible volume, with maximum bass-beat.

There were many people on the move, and bodabodas (motorbike taxis carrying up to five at a go) decided to stage outside our front door. It was incredibly noisy, but I thought I had better try to adapt, so I made myself a small, walled flower garden where I could hide away (not *quite* so noisy).

On Christmas Eve, my neighbour began to play extremely loud disco music, and planted a huge base speaker on the wall outside my bedroom window. When I went to investigate, I found he was opening a disco hall.

Throughout Christmas and New Year, there was noise as I had never known it. The iron sheets on the roof were shaking and dancing to the beat. The walls were reverberating. There was nowhere to hide. When I complained to the landlord, he pretended to become annoyed with the man. (I say he pretended because he was also the neighbour's landlord, and he had known this was going to happen.) Once or twice, when the noise was bad, he took me away to sleep in a room in his home.

Once he asked me, "What shall I do with him? Shall I shoot him?"

He was not joking. That was how that year went.

My Dutch friend Jeroon, and his wife Petwa, who had a dairy farm about a mile away, asked if I would like to use one of their cottages on Saturday nights. So, I would walk to his farm every Saturday night before dark, and pray, and I found that Jesus was really close to me on those nights.

I could still hear the noise faintly in the distance, coming from that disco, but there was peace and calm on the farm. Very early on Sunday mornings, I would go back and organise to go to church.

This 'nightclub' continued for the entire time I was in Busamaga, but in the end it failed completely, and the owner went bankrupt.

Illegal Power

I discovered dozens of cables and wires, running through the compound under the surface. Someone had made a business of stealing electricity from the main power lines, and had run cables through my compound to feed the electricity to houses down the road. Many people were being fed illegal power up the road as well, on the other side of my house. The cables were extremely dangerous, laying around, some running through puddles of water when it rained. Sadly, one child was killed when he went through water where an illegal wire had been laid. Whenever I found an illegal cable connecting to the main supply, I just cut it off.

Because of the amount of power being stolen, I found my fridge and freezer were not working properly, and so I complained to the power suppliers. I saw them come every few days, riding past my house on motorbikes, and coming back with rolls of electricity cable that they had confiscated from illegal connections. I was praised on local Kampala radio for persevering on calling them to come out to find the culprits.

Unfortunately, both my fridge and freezer were irreparably broken during this time. After I left, the power suppliers went throughout the village and gave each house a meter fed by money, and the man who had a great business supplying most of the village with illegal electricity was arrested. When the villagers found out however, they paid his fine of UGX 1,000,000 to have him released.

Looking for a Church

One Sunday, I decided to go to a church near where I lived in Busamaga. I heard the noise of the speakers, and someone playing a keyboard very badly. When I, a muzungu (white person), entered, it seemed everyone noticed, and the singing became even more of a performance. It was not what I wanted. I just wanted to worship.

I crept out and thought, *I will go home, play my guitar, read the bible, and pray there.*

As soon as I took the guitar in my hands, my dear neighbour started playing his disco noise. I was annoyed, and I decided to go and complain to the LC1 Chairman. I peeped in the neighbour's compound as I passed. He saw me and started following me. I found the LC1 was not there, but his wife was. As I began to explain to her, my neighbour began to shout, and verbally abuse me. I also began to shout, and we almost came to blows, but the Chairman's wife stood between us.

I was utterly ashamed of myself, so I left and walked along the road doing some serious thinking. I came to another church, went in, and put my head down to pray. I was disappointed and fed up with myself. When I lifted my head, the church was in the midst of raising money. People were making pledges left, right, and centre.

This is not why I came to church, I thought.

So, I left. Where should I go? I remembered a church I had passed on the way to visit Robby, a missionary friend. Reaching the church, I walked slowly towards the door. Some young girls greeted me.

"Are you coming in?" they asked. "It's a good church!"

"Is it?"

It turned out that it was an Elim Pentecostal church. They led me inside, and the worship was good. I was recognised as a visitor and was asked to greet the church.

I stood up and told them, "This morning I quarrelled with my neighbour. I am feeling very bad and ashamed of myself."

After the Word, which was beautifully delivered, I went forward for prayer, and the wife of the pastor prayed for me. She prayed exactly how I felt, and she also prayed in tongues. Something broke in me, and I wept, and wept. Then, I was completely empty. There was nothing left in me.

The Pastor's wife walked home with me because I felt that I never wanted to go back there again. At home, she braved my dogs, and sat and prayed with me in the house. What a relief to find these believers, and to be one with them.

Demands to Start a Church

I always had many visitors, with various reasons for coming to see me. Nearly all wanted prayer and money. There were several who asked me to open a Church there in Busamaga. I found myself highly resistant to their desperate pleas, knowing it was not the will of God for me.

We had a small prayer fellowship every evening in the garage, and a small meeting on Sunday mornings for those who wanted to attend. We had regular preaching around the Cross guarding the house, and quite a number received Jesus there. There were several overnight prayer meetings, and people loved to come and spend the night in my compound praying, worshiping, and listening to the Word of God. Several people came, and offered me land to build a church, but I refused. I had realised that, sadly, most people just wanted to sell land, and to profit from my stay with them.

Threat of Eviction

Nic, my son, was coming to visit me in the New Year. Oh, happy day! He was coming with his wife Mireille, and my granddaughter Marianne. I went to Entebbe to meet them at the airport.

While I was travelling to meet my family, the landlord was planning to throw out all my property from the house, and the animals from the compound. He wanted me to leave, despite the fact I had paid the rent and the utility bills were all paid up to date.

He was not happy with the animals being kept in the compound, although when we first came, he was pleased with the arrangement. He had agreed that I should remain in his house while I was looking for another place to live.

God Sends an Angel

Pastor Julius (my helper, and manager) heard about the eviction plan, and told a high security officer about it. The officer was quite annoyed by what he heard, and he came to the home with his patrol car which seated about eight soldiers behind, back-to-back. Also, he came with his two personal armed security soldiers.

They drove at high speed through the gates. The officer checked the whole compound, then went out into the market area. There he walked up and down with his armed security soldiers, in order that everyone should see him. Everyone in Busamaga knew him, and great fear descended on them.

He returned to my compound, and from that day, he posted security soldiers outside my compound every night. I was told if there was any problem at any time during the day, he would come.

The landlord, and his threats, fizzled into the background, although he continued to extort money from me for every little thing which he considered I had damaged during my tenancy. In actual fact, there was an improvement in his compound, as I had a great deal of work done on the drainage. The place used to become waterlogged when it rained, but I had worked on that.

Nevertheless, the landlord became insatiable in his demands that I pay for every little thing. That was until I informed him that if he continued, I would go to a lawyer to sort him out. Then, at last, he stopped.

Onwards with Jesus

On the day that I finally moved out, I was wearing some old socks. I took them off, shook them out, and left them hanging on the gate. As the bible says, ***If you are not welcome in any place, shake the dust off your feet, and leave.*** (Matthew 10:14)

Since that time, nobody has rented that house.

Reaping what I had Sown.

When I was looking for a new home, another of my former landlords welcomed me back with open arms. The people who were renting the property I had once rented from him, had not paid rent or utility bills for nine months, and had spoiled the house and compound.

That tenant was a mechanic, and he had turned the compound into a garage. He came with goats which ate every green thing that had been planted. The compound was filled with mechanical rubbish, and oil had been poured into the soil and the grass would not grow. Inside, he had tried to take the door handles, light fittings, wall sockets, curtain pelmets, and all the curtain tracks had been removed or damaged.

The landlord was extremely angry and wanted to prosecute him, but I believe he discovered that would be more expensive than repairing the property, and that he might never receive anything back at the end of it anyway. So, he gave up.

When I came back, the landlord told me, "This is your house, Christine."

I said, "Thank you, Jesus."

The Serere Conference

I was invited by a pastor to Serere for a leaders' discipleship conference. Pastor Christoffe had heard me teaching over the radio, and he planned for leaders to hear more. I had no money for the mission, but I told him that if the money came, I would take it as a sign that God wanted it to go ahead.

The mission was planned for a week, Monday to Friday. The Friday before it was meant to begin, the money arrived, and I set off on the Monday with Brother George Mukulu in his car. The journey was hot, and the road was dusty. It was like driving over corrugated iron sheets. We went slowly and arrived before midday.

We found the best accommodation in the Trading Centre. It was called a guest house. The rooms were small, containing one bed, one plastic basin, and a jerry can of water. There was electricity, but no internet connection. All the residents within the compound shared pit latrines. The heat increased as the day went on.

We were taken to a large, new school where we began to teach in the science laboratory. People were arriving, and they came from different churches, and denominations. Teaching was about discipleship, marriage, the Holy Spirit, and the baptism in the Holy Spirit. It was found that there was much erroneous doctrine, and cults had been trying to draw the brethren out of their true faith. There was a lack of knowledge of the scriptures. Many had never even had a bible! Knowledge of the Holy Spirit was poor.

The week went exceedingly well. There was a great change, and the Truth really set them free. It was lovely to see, and worth the discomfort, because Jesus was with us. We sent bibles for all who attended and did not own one already.

David Arrives

On Wednesday, David Livingstone arrived to help in the teaching. On Thursday something oppressed my head. I had to go back to the guest house to rest. The heat was overpowering. I took a small mattress outside to rest on, but it was not until 10pm that I normalised and was ready to preach the whole night.

The last day I was up and ready to teach and pray for the baptism in the Holy Spirit. Everyone who attended the conference received something from God. Some spoke in tongues for the first time. Some were healed, some were changed completely by the preaching and set free to become all that God wanted them to be. God was with them. It was a success.

The journey home was horribly hot, and terribly dusty. Mission accomplished!

Serere Brooks Corner 2018

Going back to teach leaders at Brooks Corner was fantastic! This time over 190 leaders attended. I went with Pastor Osika Wilberforce, Pastor Hande Julius, and Doctor George Makhulu.

I taught on servant leadership. I threw out the keyboard and loudspeakers. These instruments were being worshipped in the church at this time. I also put an end to the choir for the same reasons. I wanted us to return to God.

The brethren responded well, and the Holy Spirit was with us. They were filled with the Spirit and taught from the Bible. Many were healed and a mad woman was brought, and, under Pastor Hande's ministry, she was healed.

God impressed upon me that on the final Friday morning we should go out into the community and evangelise in pairs. It was successful – we only went for an hour but about 20 people received Jesus as their Savior. Some were also healed of long-standing problems.

As the attendees went back to their churches, the power continued with them, and even months later, there were testimonies of how the Gospel was being preached afar off. People are still being saved, and churches are being planted. God is not dead!

Looking back over the year in Busamaga it was a definite African experience! I believe we had an impact upon Busamaga.

We had good fellowship with believers in the area. There was interaction with the authorities, some of whom were corrupt; the policeman we knew was drunk most of the time. Spiritually, a number of people were saved, some healed, and some delivered from demons. Prayers were answered, and some moved away after finding work.

The Lord was with us.

Chapter 8

Mustard Seed

God's Not Dead - God Is Alive Church Ministries

It started with a Mustard Seed

The first time I went into Namatala to preach, in 1993, I went with my guitar and my first dog, Natasha. I played some praise songs which seemed to draw in a large crowd, so I stopped and preached, and some of them received Jesus.

Pastor Okumu was covering my work under Living Water Ministries, and under his watchful eye I opened the veranda on my house near Mbale Stadium for meetings. Our first Sunday service was filled to overflowing with people.

I continued to preach in Namatala, a notorious slum area where many Karamojong and Teso people live, and where there are a few 'Mugisu' (people from the tribe in the Mbale area). These Karamojong and Teso people had come from the north and were now living in that area for various reasons. Some hoped to find work, others were escaping the terrors of the rebels. Lots of them were drunkards, and amidst them were thieves and murderers. But, to all of this I was oblivious. I just preached the gospel, and they received Jesus.

One old man, Mzee, an active Church of Uganda Christian, was delighted that I had come to preach in the area. He offered me part of his land to build a church. It was God's provision. We erected a shelter with an iron sheet roof, and papyrus mats around the sides, and I held my first Sunday service there. The place was packed, and we had to double the size for the next Sunday service.

That was the beginning of Mustard Seed Church in Namatala. It was one of the first to be established; other churches had previously attempted to begin a work there but had failed.

My Assistant, Pastor Saul

I continued preaching and teaching the new converts. A student called Saul had become stuck to me as my interpreter, and we worked together. I asked someone to begin working on non-government organisation (NGO) papers, to register the church as a ministry. (Churches are not allowed to function unless they register as NGOs in Uganda). I continued to minister, while Saul went off to train as a Bible teacher at seminary for two years. When Saul returned, he became the Pastor of Mustard Seed Church, Namatala.

Before Saul left for seminary, he had become the ward of a girl whose mother was a local pastor. A sponsorship paid for the child's education, and the money for this came through my bank account. To ensure a level of accountability, I was regularly kept informed regarding the progression of her studies (an added motivation for her to do well). My suspicions were aroused however, when one day I saw her wearing high heel shoes and carrying a mobile phone.

Unfortunately, I did not have any opportunity to see her again for a long time after that.

This same girl had lived in my house with her mother for quite a long time when she and her mother had no accommodation. She was a difficult girl, and her mother was unable to control her.

Much later I found out she was continuing her studies, but also that she had given birth to, and was raising, Saul's child. Up until that point, Saul, the girl, and her mother, had kept the pregnancy and birth hushed up, well enough to keep the church, and me, in total ignorance.

The church stood Saul down as pastor. He was utterly downcast, ashamed, and sorry, and after a long while he was re-instated as pastor. Saul went on to marry the girl, perhaps out of a sense of obligation, but it was not what God wanted.

Until this all happened, we had been very close. I loved Saul dearly and had invested a great deal of trust in him, and time and effort into aiding his spiritual growth and in supporting his ministry.

It was not Saul's sin that hurt me most, though I was terribly disappointed he had let the church, himself, and the Lord, down in that way, but rather it was his deceiving me, and for such a long period of time too. That took me an awfully long time to recover from.

This true story is a reminder, that even if we have God's forgiveness, sin often still results in serious, or even life-long, inescapable consequences. It has ruined reputations, relationships, families, and much more besides. All of us carry the scars of our own, and of other people's sinful words and actions.

Luring us in with promises of instant gratification, sin ensnares and enslaves its victims, keeping us longer than we wanted to stay, and costing us much more than we thought we would pay. Our sin is the reason the Saviour had to be tortured and hung on a cross, to die a humiliating and agonising death. It is no light matter.

Sin pulls us away from God and from salvation, and ultimately if we do not turn to the Lord and repent, it leads us straight to hell.

Pastor Peter Clifton-Sprigg

Pastor Peter Clifton-Sprigg started working on a Bible School project, and came to Uganda frequently, and with his wife at the last. I was devastated when he and his family left Uganda in a hurry, because his life had been threatened. He had deviated from the calling laid upon him, and had begun a restaurant business.

I remember assisting in the baptism of students from Peter's school. It was so powerful. Most of the candidates had to be carried out of the water, slain in the Holy Spirit. Many of them were speaking in tongues.

Even now, all these years on, I grieve over him. I think he lost his way. I am so sorry.

Pastor Richard

After Saul, the church had another Pastor, the late Richard from Teso. Pastor Richard was highly anointed, and he was one of the first group of students to be taught by the late Peter, at the Peter Clifton-Spriggs Bible School.

Pastor Richard was going on well with the Church in Namatala, when he went for a visit to the UK. It was then that he tried to bring the Mustard Seed ministry under another ministry there. The Pastor of that ministry knew me and alerted me to what was happening. It became clear to me that Richard was trying to sell the church, the cows belonging to the Church, the land, the building, and even the church furniture!

When he arrived back, I told him, "Go back to your village in Dokolo!"

Lots of the brethren in the Church were angry with me; Pastor Richard was a very charismatic person, and they loved him. However, he still went away, which resulted in some of our church members leaving and beginning another fellowship.

We all make mistakes, and despite being hurt by Richard's actions in the UK, I soon regained a respect for him. He left when I asked him to, and carried on the Lord's work, preaching the gospel, and planting many churches in his area. His people called him Bishop, and I am happy to acknowledge that he went on to achieve something great for the Lord.

On one occasion, I was accused of having a bad relationship with Richard. After hearing that, I called him and asked, "Is there anything that you have against me?"

With a voice of sincerity, he replied, "Certainly not!"

I perceived a real bond of Christ's love between us, and I was sorry when he later became ill with diabetes. He became blind, and died, but up until this day I love him, and believe we shall meet in Heaven.

The Ministry

There have been numerous complications with Mustard Seed Church in Namatala, but God has been with us in a powerful way. We have seen many signs and wonders.

Pius

Pius, a Karamojong, was a street boy, who started, and finished school in Primary 1. He could not read nor write, however God had helped him to sign his name.

He signed something for me once. putting the pen down, he said, "The pen was very heavy today."

Someone gave Pius a Bible written in Karamojong, and though unable to read anything else, he found that he could read that Bible from Genesis to Revelation!

He used to walk, selling small items. One day, as he passed a party of Gisu, dancing and drumming up their gods whilst taking a boy for circumcision, a vehicle knocked Pius down. He was badly injured. His head swelled up, and when he came to church, he was on crutches; his broken arms and legs covered in plaster of Paris.

Pius asked me to pray for his healing, which I did. He was so depressed that he decided to go back to Karamoja and die. The doctor in the hospital in Mbale had told him that his arm must be amputated. And at this news, he ran away.

He was in his village, seated in one of the grass huts with a few people, when lightning struck. He was thrown out of the house, up into the air, and came down with a huge blow. He went to a hospital in Karamoja. He was completely healed! All the fractures were healed… How God loves him!

His sons were brilliant at school and always 1st in their class. They had the ability to reach University standard. Pius himself told me that he always wanted to be a doctor. I believe he was a slow learner due to malnutrition in his infancy.

Death and Demons

We had to bury a Karamojong who died in Namatala. The grave was dug in the church ground. It was all so undignified. All the leaders in the church were away, and I had to conduct the burial.

They wrapped the body in a sheet, and came running down the road with it, and placed it in the grave. I began to pray for all the people who had to deal with this. The corpse was not known. He had arrived off the bus the previous night to stay with someone in Namatala. Then he died. I found someone tugging at my skirt.

It was my deacon, kneeling there saying, "Sister, pray for me. I am very sick!"

As I prayed for him, he vomited into the grave. That was a demon that had entered him from the body. After burial everyone was heavy in spirit and miserable. I took them into the church and prayed for all of them. The oppression lifted. The demons of death departed.

We praised, we thanked God, and we left in good spirits.

Miracles and Growth

One lady had suffered from AIDS for years, and she was taking ARVs. God healed her. Others were healed from all sorts of diseases commonly found in Africa. Many were saved. Some have grown under discipleship to become ministers.

Others still have left the church and moved on. They have taken the Gospel with them. (Town churches have a big turnover!)

A sister church was planted in Namabasa. Pastor Phillip Lotimong became the pastor. It grew strong and healthy. I discipled them for two years.

Trials and Tribulations

Pastor Saul continued to lead Mustard Seed church, Namatala, from the time of Pastor Richard, until the 2020s, when he handed it over to me. Until then, during late 2015-19, I was preaching once a month in Mustard Seed Church.

There were one or two issues that I was not happy about. Pastor Saul was not willing to change his policy on interpretation. The sermons used to be translated into Ateso, as Tesot and Karamojong understood that language, and there were more of these tribes in the church. Saul wanted the sermons to be in Luganda, which was understood by his Gisu tribe. Also, I sensed some tribalism coming into the church.

Another problem was the attire of the worship leader (the wife of Saul). It was proud, provocative, and in fact it was all about *Look At Me*!!

I asked Saul for more time to be with the church and to teach them, which was denied. I wrote to inform him that I was leaving the church. I said that I would not stop him, or interfere with what he wanted, but I was leaving. I let the whole matter go and left him to it.

Soon after this a storm came and blew the roof off the church. Saul's mother-in-law's house fell whilst she was inside it. She was rescued but sustained a serious back injury.

More Trouble

This was not the end of the troubles for Mustard Seed Church. You may remember the brother who had given the land for the church way back in 1993. Well, he died, and his children decided they wanted the land of the church back if I was no longer leading the church.

There was a terrible battle over the land, and Pastor David Livingstone was injured in a physical fight. Pastor Saul took the case to a court of law. I stood by and watched.

Another leader, Pastor Okotel of Light House

Church, came in to try to negotiate the case out of court. The family of the original owner of the land was calling me to witness for them. My heart was with the church, but I came in as neither on one side nor the other. I prayed, and God gave me the scripture 1 Corinthians 6:7, which says that it is better to suffer being wronged than to take your brothers to court.

I talked to the church leaders and gave them the scripture. God wanted them to let it go. At first they could not allow it, but as we persisted, one-by-one, they let it go. David Livingstone found it most difficult, but in the end, he released it with great sorrow. Pastor Saul threw himself on the ground and wept, and at the last, he too gave up the land.

I had bought a second piece of land from the brother who gave us the first piece. At that time, in 1993, I had a pickup vehicle which I sold to buy the land for the ministry, so we decided we should transfer the church to this second piece of land.

The original owners tried to fight for this as well, but failed.

It was terrible transferring the old buildings, the fence etc. I was really upset. Writing this even now, I am close to tears as I recall the situation.

The late Marion, a dear friend, had left money to build a Sunday school. It was an excellent building, and up to British standard; one brother had even come over from England just to fix the electrical wiring. It had been used by the children that Marion loved.

Also, Pastor Okotel started his first sponsored school in the building.

It was demolished. The whole building… Gone forever.

David Livingstone worked with frenzy and erected a huge iron-sheet church on the land we had retained. About this time, Pastor Saul was stuck by a serious spinal problem. His legs were paralysed, and he was in pain and discomfort, and he received treatment in several locations.

A Transferral and A Transformation

I believe God wanted me to go and pray with him when he was in a hospital in Kumi. So I went, and I managed to speak to him on his own, telling him what I believed God wanted me to say. He wept and I prayed for his healing. I really thought he was going to be healed, but it never happened. However, he did regain the use of his legs to an extent and began walking with a limp.

It was soon after this, Saul told me that he was handing the church in Namatala back to me. That is when…

I took over as Overseer (for Life).

God is Alive ministries started.

The land title was bought.

The ministry registered with the government.

We prayed over the constitution, and it was given to us from the Bible.

From there, it has been exceedingly difficult to change the ways of the *'old church'* into being led by the *'new constitution.'* The new way is actually the original way that the first century church was in the beginning at Antioch. Basically, we are following Jesus to go into all the world, preach the Good News, Baptise in the Name of the Father, the Son, and the Holy Spirit, make disciples, and Jesus has promised to be with us, and that we will speak in tongues, heal the sick, cast out demons, and not die when we drink poison or step on snakes, and scorpions!!!!

We believe in Holy marriage and Holy Communion. We are trying to follow Jesus. There is no turning back.

Some have left the church because it has changed. More than a few new people have come, and are still coming. Pastor Julius Hande is the Senior Pastor of the ministry. He is an ex-prisoner who has many churches and fellowships, especially in the Mooni area.

Also, we have a church in Kidongole, which is being led by Pastor Felix, an ex-prisoner, a church in Budadiri, and yet another next to my home in Namabasa.

Pastor Hande has a powerful healing and miracle ministry, and we have seen endless signs and wonders, and we are seeing people converted, which is wonderful.

A lot of converts bring difficulties for us, however. Provisions need to be made when they are thrown out of their homes, for accommodation, food, clothing, and work. Such converts often come with children - which means they need to cover school fees. Some also come with health problems and so need treatment; many are infected with HIV. We are always crying unto our God for more provision for the needy.

The ministry is to the poor...We are told to take the Gospel to the poor.

Chapter 9

Travelling Turmoil

These days, in 2024, life in Ugandan towns and cities these days is quite civilised. Uganda has developed incredibly since I arrived in 1990. There are beautiful buildings and tower blocks in Kampala, and many expensive luxury hotels in Jinja, Entebbe, and other cities.

Taxis, buses, and bodabodas are the main means of public transport, but Ugandan taxis are usually not 5-seater cars that transport people locally, they are mini-buses used for travelling from city to city. These taxis have both a driver, and a conductor who touts for passengers. He loads the passengers three to four people crammed into three seats - along with luggage bags, sacks of produce, and live chickens, all inside, and up on the top of the vehicle. It may take an hour or so for the taxi to fill to the point at which no-one else can be squeezed in, and only when the conductor is satisfied that the taxi's load has reached its absolute limits does the journey begin. Usually, these journeys are fast, and dangerous.

The last time I travelled from Kampala to Mbale by taxi was about 10 years ago. The driver was driving like a maniac, so I complained, and asked him to reduce his speed. He slowed up a little for about five minutes, but then went back to speeding. His demons were driving us!

When we reached Jinja, I decided I would alight there and wait for another vehicle. However, the conductor asked if I was going to Mbale, and then refused to allow me to get off. I was seriously annoyed. It was almost a kidnap! Once more I explained that the driver was driving too fast, but still the conductor forced me to remain in the taxi.

The driver started to feel guilty and reduced his speed, but instead of being sensible, he went to the other extreme, and drove the whole of the remaining 130 miles at 30mph! It was painfully slow.

I was seething in the back seat, and thinking how I was going to handle the driver at the end of the journey. I thought, *I may not pay him… I will report him to the police… I will really lash him with my tongue…*

But then God spoke to me, saying, "Forgive him."

When we reached Mbale, I walked over to the driver and said, "You have been very bad. I felt that I should not pay you. Why have you treated me like this? Is it because I am a woman? Or because I am a muzungu (white)? I wanted to report you to the police, but God has spoken to me and told me to forgive you."

The other passengers all sided with me, and in a show of agreement they cheered loudly. I told God that I would never travel by taxi again, and that I would never leave Mbale again, unless I had enough money to go by car.

A Terrible Accident

Another time, I was escorting my visitors, Jim and Norma Gregory, back from Entebbe. We stopped at a traffic light in Kampala, and on our side of the road there were empty taxis in a row for quite a distance, all parked one behind another. There was a street boy coming out between the taxis, trying to find a place to cross the road safely. He would take a look, retreat, then appear again, coming out between other taxis, still looking for a gap in the traffic.

A speeding taxi suddenly appeared, pulling in to join the end of the line of empty taxis. He was travelling so fast however, that he didn't have time to brake properly, and slammed into the back of the last taxi in the row. The impact sent it ricocheting forward into the next vehicle, which hit the one in front, and so on, all the way down the line of parked taxis. There was no time for the boy to react or to get out of the way! He was crushed and then thrown up from between two of the taxis. He twirled in the air and then he fell to the ground. It all happened so fast that I actually thought I saw two boys.

A policeman was there at the time. He assessed the situation and told us, "He's gone."

It was all so sudden - we were in shock. The boy had been killed right in front of our eyes. I remember seeing his sandals on the road and wondering, why had I seen two boys? It was all so dreadful, especially for my dear friend Norma.

The Main Road

Uganda is land-locked, with vehicles coming from Kenya, Congo, and everywhere else. The roads have always been bad, even now in 2024, especially when travelling from Iganga to Kampala on the main road, which leads from many different border points into Uganda. This road is used by heavy goods vehicles, buses, taxis, cars etc. Trucks make their way from one country to another, trundling along slowly through Africa with their loads of petrol and everything else. But this 'main road' has only two lanes, one heading East, and the other West, and along the way there are frequent police check points. As you may imagine, traffic can be a real nightmare!

Modern Kampala

Back in 1990, it was easy to travel to travel from Kamuli, through Jinja, to Kampala. The journey might have taken only an hour and a half there, and the same going back.

I could relax in Kampala for a few hours and have an ice-cream – something which is not available in the villages where I lived. I could go to a supermarket - one large room filled with goodies, some of which were not available in the villages.

It was the only supermarket that I knew of in Uganda, and it was owned by Kenyans. There was the large Sheraton Hotel, where I could buy a cream cake, and have a cup of coffee.

Today however, although you may be stuck in a traffic jam for three or four hours, Kampala is a big, beautiful city with all amenities, and there are now many real supermarkets and big hotels.

But you have not seen Uganda if you have only been to Kampala. The further north you travel, the more you will see the real life of this country. It is a very hard place for most people to live.

No Alternative Route!

I remember travelling back to Mbale from Entebbe with David Ardron, many years ago. When we reached Iganga, we stopped at the end of a long queue of traffic. Up ahead, the road was flooded. A bridge had broken.

David took out a map to look for an alternative route. Then he realised - there was no alternative route. We were in Africa!

Near the broken bridge, some men were directing small cars and taxis to turn left, off the road. After a few meters the vehicles were being guided through a small stream. We followed behind a taxi. As the taxi entered the water, the back end rose up in front of us. It had reached a dip in the stream. I wanted to jump out and walk through, but we had begun and there was no turning back. Men on either side of the car helped us to get through.

The car suffered a little water damage, but the engine was okay. We turned right, through the grass, and at last managed to reach the road on the other side of the broken bridge. The rest of the journey home was uneventful.

Bodabodas - Motorbike Taxis

The most dangerous vehicle on the roads in Uganda is used by thousands of people every day. More than a hundred people die every week in bodaboda accidents in Kampala alone. Many more are injured, and some die from their injuries later. I never feel safe, even walking on the side of the road, because of these motorbike taxis. In Mbale the death rate is high from Bodabodas accidents.

When I came to Uganda, the bodabodas were all pedal bicycles with a cushion seat on the back. Ladies sat side-saddle, and men sat astride. Once, when I was in Jinja, I flagged a bodaboda.

When he saw me, he said, "You are too heavy."

I was annoyed, and I told him, "You sit, and I will ride you."

He sat, and for the first time in my life, I tried to start off with a man on the cushion seat.

He said, "Go! Push hard!"

I pushed on the pedals, and we were off! I rode him to my destination, and then requested that he pay me… (it never happened!)

I was often taken into the villages on the backs of these bicycles. It was lovely riding along narrow paths and under cool trees, and looking up at the blue, blue sky. Many birds sang in the trees, and huge, beautiful butterflies fluttered past. At night, travelling home in the dark after a day of ministry in evangelism and discipleship, our path was lit by myriads of fireflies. Enchanting!

Sadly, we do not see the butterflies or the fireflies today. But even if they were still around as they used to be, they would go mostly unnoticed, as nearly everyone is rushing as fast as possible on these horrible motorbike bodabodas.

Soon after the motorbike bodabodas started arriving in Uganda, I felt God was telling me never to ride on them. I had already seen a bodaboda driver splayed out dead on the road before me, as I was travelling near the dam in Jinja.

Then my doctor advised me not to ride on the bodabodas. She saw in an X-ray that my bones were becoming thin. At the same time the British High Commission was heard advising Brits not to ride on the bodabodas. All in all, I had received a strong message from my doctor, my Queen, and, above all, my God. So, I stopped.

People have spoken against me for not using bodabodas. One bodaboda driver told me, "You fear to die."

I responded, "I don't fear to die. I fear God."

I have never had enough money to buy and maintain a car, and I walk almost everywhere I go. I believe that God wants me to walk.

Greetings and the Gospel

Uganda has about 40 languages, but most people use Luganda, or Swahili. English is the official language of the country; you will always find someone around who speaks English.

When I am out, I may greet people, saying, "How are you?" in Lugandan, "Oli otya?" or in

Swahili, "Habari?" or, "Jamb?", or in the local Lugisu language, "Mirembe?"

Ugandans say that visitors are all welcome, and that you may be receiving angels when you entertain them! Everyone in Uganda is friendly. Everyone greets on the way, and those who don't greet others are regarded as very rude.

This custom helps, as I usually meet people and find I am easily able to talk to them. Much of my evangelism happens when I talk to the people as I am walking.

Passing the stage for the taxis, the conductors often ask me, "O genda wa?" (Where are you going?)

I reply, "Nyenda mu Gulu." (I am going to Heaven.) "O genda wa?" (Where are YOU going?)

It is a good way to start a Gospel message.

Busy Busses

Buses are also used a lot in Uganda. They are very big vehicles, which are usually driven everywhere at excessive speeds, with the driver honking the horn to ensure all other drivers make way for the King of the Road! Passengers ride on a high level, while luggage is packed in a large compartment under the seating. The seats are small; measured for pygmies, I think.

It is usually hot, and the air is thick with smells of sweat, cheap perfume, and of the foods people are often eating as they travel. Stops are made to buy cooked chicken on sticks with cooked sweet-bananas (gonja), sodas and water. Live chickens and turkeys, and all kinds of fruits are also on sale at the side of the roads.

The Big Race

There was once a time when two big buses were making the journey north to Soroti, at the same time. Legend has it that a race began…Two big buses hurtling side by side, the passengers urging each driver on! I know not who won, BUT the Ugandans certainly enjoyed it.

These days, inside the bus is a TV screen, which plays loud music and shows the evocative dancing that Ugandans love.

There are not many bus accidents, but when there is, usually a lot of people die. Our Administrator, Fred Masakala, was in a bus accident when he was travelling to Kampala. He found himself standing on the roof of the bus, which had been sliced off! He appeared to be okay, and, somehow, his bag was with him. Later, some internal bleeding was found, and his spleen had to be removed. But. other than that, he was totally fine.

Many of the passengers died, and even more were seriously injured, and we have always wondered what happened to Fred. How was he saved? How did he suddenly find himself standing on the severed top of the bus relatively unharmed and with his belongings? It was a miracle.

It would be really difficult for me to make a journey on one of these buses now, even if it is a quick way to travel.

Chapter 10

Photos

1991

A month of mission in Kabale

Kabale 1991

Kabale 1991

2015 trip to UK, to see my son Tim, daughter in law Linda, and granddaughter Emily.

My son Nic, his wife Mireille, a pastor and me, at my home in Uganda in 2014.

Marianne, my granddaughter with me, when her family visited Uganda in 2014.

Sweet William, my helper in the compound, expert at finding lost glasses, and mobile phones.

Christine with God is Alive Church, Namatala.

This baby was miraculously raised from the dead, through prayer, in the name of the Jesus.

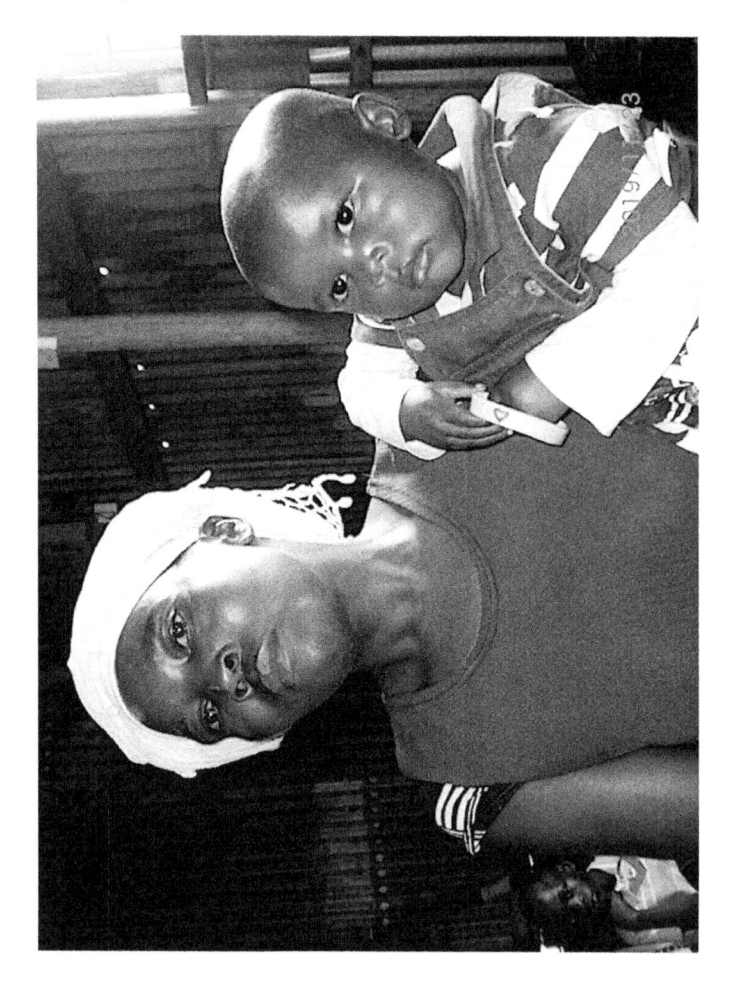

Beautiful children in the slums of Namatala, Mbale.

Moses graduated from keeping my cows, to graduation!

Dear friends from the Church of Uganda. Bishop Gimadu and his wife Ruth, on the way to minister at Mooni God is Alive Church.

Workers in Karamoja, on land given by the government to Pius.

In Margaret's room with some of her children, after her husband died.

Faith Radio with Jim and Sylvia

Jack carrying children at a party at one of the hotels.

My beautiful Polly (dog) and beautiful Bishop (cat) at Christmas. Faithful friends, now departed.

Christine Centre in a village near Tororo, after teaching discipleship seminars.

The Author, Me!

A Place to call Home

A few years ago, I moved from a rented property on the edge of town, just a kilometre from the centre of Mbale city, to a village about five kilometres away from the city.

Until then, I had rented the whole time I had been in Uganda, because there was never anything like enough money to even consider buying land, or for building. All my money was spent, almost as soon as I received it, on paying bills, paying workers, money for ministry (transport accommodation on mission, airtime for radio, needs of the prisoners, needs of the poor in church), and on every other problem that came to my door on an almost daily basis.

Owning my own home here in Uganda is not something I considered necessary for a long time. When I started off, I was content to sleep on the floor of a mud hut, whatever was needed to minister to the people here.

But after decades of bad renting experiences, such as threats of eviction, antisocial and highly disruptive neighbours, rent suddenly being raised extortionately, extra fees being demanded and new charges being invented, I concluded that the Lord's money, and my time and energies, were being constantly wasted.

I realised that only owning my own property could resolve all of this. I hadn't thought it possible though, given the insatiable demands of the ministry, the never-ending needs of the people around me, and my financial limitations. But God is a God of the impossible, and He has no limitations.

Jehovah Jirah, My Provider

About three years ago, God touched the heart of a faithful supporter called William, who lives in Scotland. He was very concerned that I did not own a house here in Uganda, and he bought land, and built a house for me in Namabasa, where I now live. When I calculated the cost, it was about the equivalent of the whole 30 years of renting. What a miracle!

God has blessed me so much. After renting houses for 28 years in Uganda, a brother in the UK sent me money to buy land, and to build a house. It was a miracle. May God bless William in Scotland whom I have never met, but whom God spoke to about me, and who was obedient.

I never ever had enough money to save, or to build. Everything that was given to me was used for my basic needs, and the remaining part has always been used to help the poor. That was what God wanted. But now, it is so relieving to have a permanent home that I own outright, so that I can now focus entirely on the ministry and the needs of others, rather than waste the resources I have on dubious and often infuriating landlords, trying to extort me for every shilling I have.

I realise that most people around the world will never own a home of their own, even in the UK the housing market out-prices many, including those with full time jobs. I am truly blessed and am thankful for this answer to prayer. Seek First the Kingdom of God, and All These Things Shall be Added Unto You. (Matthew 6:33)

So, I moved to the village. There was no electricity and no water, and Matthew went every day on our donkey and cart to collect water from a bore hole near a mosque, for the animals and for cleaning. I bought drinking water in a jerry can from a tap and boiled it. I think I was using a charcoal stove for cooking until I had enough money to buy a gas cooker. What a blessing that was!

Going Electric

Later, God blessed me with enough money to buy Solar. It was wonderful to have light, and power for the internet and charging phones. On a good hot sunny day I could use my blender to make a glass of juice, and my hand mixer to mix some cake. Before that I think I was using candles, and a couple of oil lamps.

I never bought a fridge. I lived for a long time in Uganda without a fridge when I first came. I learned how to keep food from going off by boiling and through other methods.

We make enough for today… Today, I fill a big saucepan with sand, and then completely saturate the sand with water. I put a small saucepan in the centre of the sand, and put in the yoghurt, jam, or any little thing to keep cool. It is kept under the sink, in the coolest place. The heat is kept from the inner pan by the surrounding water, which evaporates as it warms up, taking the heat with it. When the water level in the sand is reduced, we simply top it up with more. It is an economical and relatively simple way to keep a few perishable items cool enough for a day or so.

Locals believe that it was because I am living here that electricity came to Namabasa! I have found favour here, but not everyone likes the whites, or *muzungu* as they are called here. Whites are very welcome when they come with money to help with projects, but then it is time for them to go home.

I became a citizen of Uganda primarily because I wanted to be on a par with the people I was living and working with. I felt, as a visitor, I was not able to say ALL that I wanted. But now, as a citizen, I can speak as a Ugandan, and I feel that my words carry more authority and weight than they did before.

The Blessing of Water

I contacted Uganda National Water and Sewerage, and I managed to have approximately 300 metres of pipe installed and connected. The people in my area all managed to connect as well. They were pleased to say the least, and I gained favour among the villagers.

It was a Muslim area and Christians were not well tolerated. My neighbour was an LC, (a local government leader), and she was very happy with me for bringing water, and for coming to live in the area. She told me that some years ago, a white woman came into the area to evangelise. She was abused by the locals, and she spoke something like a curse over them all. From that time, nothing went well. The LC saw me as one who had come to break the curse.

The white woman she was talking about was an elderly lady called Marion from the Mansfield area in Britain. I knew her. She became ill in Uganda and was taken back to the UK, where she died. Marion helped many people in Uganda and was usually a happy soul. She had left a legacy which built a Sunday school next to our church in Namatala. At one stage, the charity 'Child of Hope' used the facility when they started their school.

Village Life

Today, in 2024, although there are still mud huts in Uganda, the country has developed significantly. Most people in the villages live in brick and cement dwellings with corrugated iron roofs, though some have mud floors, and some have mud walls.

Fabulous Food (if you can Afford it)

Although there is much poverty, and much hardship everywhere you look, Uganda is actually very rich in natural food. Everything is grown here, including sugar, tea, and coffee. Meat sources are usually cows, goats, and chickens. Tilapia fish comes from Lake Victoria, and Nile Perch from the River Nile. It is no wonder Uganda is called the Pearl of Africa!

In Mbale, smoked bamboo is eaten, and is considered a delicacy, but I am not fond of it - I taste only smoke.

The fruits and vegetables are gorgeous - the tomatoes, onions, cabbages, sukuma wik (thick green leaves like cabbages, but they are delicious), as well as peas and avocados. There are also melons, green oranges, mangoes, bananas, jack fruit (a huge, green, thick-skinned fruit, with sticky yellow flesh inside that is extremely sweet (I love it, BUT you become so sticky that if you tried to kiss someone, you would be stuck together!)

Most food is eaten with groundnut paste, cooked maize flour, millet, sorghum, cassava, soya beans, all kinds of other beans (brown, black, greenish white), matooke (cooked banana), rice, and sweet and 'Irish' potatoes.

It is common for people to keep chickens and goats. Wealthier people have cows. Pigs are not seen in this Muslim area, but they are kept in Namatala where there's a 'Pork Joint'. This is loved by many Ugandans. It is a place to drink beer, eat pork, and enjoy the company of others.

It is June as I write this, and here in the village, people are lacking food, but the bean harvest is just coming in and they will soon have enough. In about a month the maize harvest will also come in. The staple diet is maize flour and beans, and up in the mountainous area, bananas for cooking, called matooke.

Sadly, western living has crept in, with its highly processed and unhealthy foods, and as a result people are now suffering and dying from western diseases, such as diabetes, high blood pressure, heart attacks, cancer, ulcers, TB, and so on. These all add to the list of diseases Uganda was already struggling to cope with, top of the list being things like Malaria, and HIV/AIDS, which seems to be more prevalent than ever.

Drinking

Many of the villagers, like most Ugandans, are great drinkers of local beer, drunk from a large clay pot, with what looks to me like sewage floating on the top!

This highly alcoholic drink is made locally, and is loved. Men sit around the pot with long straws, drinking and putting the world to rights. They may spend all day, and all night, around this small god, despite the fact it causes death, poverty, and bad relationships…

I think this may be a world-wide problem.

Unholy Covenants

Every tribe has its own culture. Where I live, all boys have to be circumcised in a cultural way. This involves the child dressing in monkey-skin hat, beads across the chest, a banana fibre skirt, and carrying a stick with a white monkey tail on the end.

The boys are plied with a great deal of alcohol, and they are carried on the shoulders of men who dance amid a crowd of people to the beat of tribal drums. They dance for hours; eyes glaze over as demons take control. Each boy's skin is covered in white. Then they are taken to dance on the graves of their 'jajas' - grandmothers. After this, they drink a drug and then eagerly desire to 'face the knife.' Only special tribal 'doctors,' with dedicated knives, perform these operations.

Just as they cut the boy, they sacrifice a goat, removing its heart and lifting it up on a pole. The candidate has been given in a blood sacrifice to Musambwa (just another name for the devil), their (so-called) god, who is said to dwell on Mount Elgon. After this there is feasting, drinking, and debauchery. Thus, are all Bagisu given to the devil. The demons in the men are transferred, through physical intimacy, to the women. Because of this demonic blood covenant, it has always been exceedingly difficult for this tribe to receive salvation. Blood covenants are very strong, and I have opposed this ritual all the years I have been here.

Every Knee Shall Bow, and Every Tongue Confess

However, God has given me the desire of my heart, which was to see people from this tribe, and others like it, being born again. Many have now received Jesus as their Lord and Saviour. That is what gives me the greatest satisfaction. Also, I love to see people grow in salvation through discipleship, and to find their Holy calling in the Lord Jesus Christ.

Prison is the place where a lot of people find and receive Jesus. God opened the prison ministry to me from the time that I arrived in Uganda. I have prayed with, and discipled, prisoners once a week, for 31 years. (The other two years we were not allowed into prison because of Covid.)

Chapter 11

Prison Ministry

When I skyped my son Nic in New Zealand, I found him sitting with Benjamin his son. Nic was bemoaning the fact that he was getting old! At that time Benjamin was about 25, and Nic had reached the ripe old age of 54.

When they asked me what I was doing, I said, "Fridays is my day of personal prayer, and preparation. On Saturdays I pray with the leaders, and make a broadcast from 9-10pm. Sundays I am in church, after the main service I teach the youth, and the worship team. Monday mornings there is a pastors' fellowship ending with breakfast at about 1pm. Tuesdays, I am in prison…"

"Grandma!" exclaimed Benjamin, then he asked me twice over, "What are you doing in prison?"

"I am teaching them and discipling them." I replied, and a look of relief passed over his face.

Yes, I have been going to prison weekly for the past 31 years, having the privilege of witnessing lives transformed by the power of the Truth of the Gospel of Jesus Christ, week after week, and year after year. It has been, and it still is, truly wonderful!

Here is a testimony from one of the prisoners I prayed with in 1993 in Mbale. He had been sentenced to death with some others, and I was asked to pray with them.

My testimony from Death Row

Born in 1970. In 1981 I joined the army and served for five years. I was arrested in 1991 under suspicion of being the leader of a group of soldiers where one member shot the man who was selling bullets to the Karamojong Warriors in Moroto. Before that man was killed we tried to arrest him. He tried to run, and escape and one of the group shot him. Six of us were arrested including the one who shot the man. We were taken to court which ruled the incident was punishable by DEATH for it was a murder case. While in prison three out of the six were released, and became the witnesses pinning the case on us. Finally in 1994 I was sentence to death by the High Court with my companions. We appealed but it was ruled no change could be made other than death by hanging.

Before entering the Condemned Section, the President had signed for 20 inmates to be executed. That was Luzira Upper Prison, 1991. In the Condemned Section, I knew that I was going to die one day in 1996 when another group of 19 people were executed. I witnessed it with my own eyes. It was the same year the Judges called my file to confirm that I would be included in the next execution. That year I appealed my case to the President.

There were thirty five of us. We knew that after every three years execution had to take place. With a lot of fear I exclaimed, "Mungu Wangu" meaning 'O my God', and with devotion I used the book of Isaiah 43:1-3 which says He will be with me.

(Thanks be to God a school was opened in Luzira Prison, and I started in Primary 2 up to Primary 7.) Then in 1999 another execution was organized with 28 inmates to be executed, and one of whom was my best friend in the prison, my classmate, and brother in Faith. The one responsible came and called the names. If someone was to be hanged he was directed where to go, and if you are to be released, also directed you where to go. By God's Mercy, I did not hear my name.

After reading the names the door was locked, and those whose names had been read had to be taken away. After about four minutes the one responsible came and opened my ward, and called MR BATARINGAYA, my best friend, and the leader in the ward. One day he had raised a false accusation against us that we wanted to take up his power. We were called to Reception to answer the case, but the phone rang, and we told to meet in the afternoon. In the afternoon he had names of those to be executed. O my God, there my friend's name BATARINGAYA appeared. As they were taking him to be executed, I cried endlessly for my friend is going to be killed without confessing the words he wanted to say while at the Reception. From that I learned a lesson that you should not raise a false witness against a brother out of anger, or anything. Among those on which my friend was numbered were 28 inmates, and 16 to be pardoned by being convicted to 20 years in prison with remission.

All those 13 and a half years I used to pray like this: O GOD CAN YOU RESERVE ME FOR

SOME MORE YEARS, THAT I MAY CONTINUE TO TESTIFY ABOUT YOUR GOODNESS, POWER, AND YOUR STRONG WEAPONS THAT YOU USE UPON MY ENEMIES.

Thanks be to God I continued my studies in prison up to Senior 4.

On 16th March 2006, the President pardoned 16 inmates, and my name did not appear at all. I kept asking myself "Why me?" Some of my friends with whom I appealed were executed, and others not. I remained crying, because in my ward we remained as few as 35 inmates. After that some were taken to be executed. We remained 6. Uhhh!

It was on a bright day on 4th March 2002, when my name appeared on the list of those to be executed. There were 43 inmates including those from other wards. IMAGINE? It was on that note that Rev Fr TARCISIO AGOSTONI fought for me. Really, I became worried. A miracle happened - we were not taken for execution.

As we were waiting execution in 1999 we had organised points to endorse in order to fight the death penalty, but this was kind of taking a risk, because even the Ministers at that time did not agree with us. Also some of my fellow inmates refused to sign, because of fear. There were rumours that nobody should agree to abolish the death penalty. So it was not an easy job. But easy with God!

We were through. It started slowly that nobody should be executed before finishing the final judgements from the court. Then our lawyers also did a great job to sensitize people about these points. Thanks for the government to allow the sensitisation in this season, There were other hangings carried out until the Human Rights ministry condemned it on 29th April 2002 until 20th May 2005 when the Court of Appeal ruled out that no one should be executed after being in Condemned Section for more than three years. After the dismissal in the court, he would not die by hanging. I praise God, because I had stayed in the prison for 18 years.

In prison I used 2 Corinthians 1:10-11 and Psalm 102:19-24. I prayed that God should save my life because I am still young. Jeremiah 33:3. I jumped up while singing, "Jesus set me free," and, "Katonda ayamba nga embilo kwotudde."

Stand firm in Christ, and believe that it is through the Blood of Jesus that I am out of Condemned Section.

I would like to thank Jesus who enlightened our DEAR President to pardon us, and I thank him for life imprisonment where I have hope for the future.

God is alive, and is still with us.

By Frederick Mukhama, son of Mr Joseph Wanyera

Fred Mukhama was released from prison and is serving as a Pastor. Now, here are some details of the prison ministry, life in prison etc.

Awful Conditions

After three years I began going into the Mbale Prison and ministering to the prisoners there. It was nothing like we imagine prison over in the UK. Only the most basic of necessities are provided, a little maize flour, beans, and water.

The prisoners were given two meals a day of maize flour, which was of the lowest grade, and often bitter, and beans badly cooked. There is no salt, and plenty of weevils.

No medicines were available, regardless of how sick an inmate might become, and they were dying from diseases that can be easily treated. Rosemary, a lady from the UK, sent money to buy the prisoners medicine, with which a great number of lives were saved, through receiving common drugs for malaria, infections, and diarrhoea. I was able to supply the medicine through such kind donations for many years, thank the Lord.

The uniforms were in tatters. Inmates often used their own trousers which also ended up in rags. There was no access to clean clothing.

Prisoners slept on concrete floors in long wards of 100 people. They were never given a mattress, and they had only one worn out, grubby, thin blanket each to sleep with.

The prisoners were beaten frequently, even by their fellow prisoners.

Often the prisoners are incarcerated for years, for the most insignificant, minor or even unprovable offences, without either witnesses or evidence. There is a great deal of corruption and bribery in the system.

Sometimes prisoners try to escape. It is usually when the rain is there, and they have been taken out on work parties. I was there on a couple of occasions when there was an escape. Guns are fired at the escapees, and occasionally they are killed. If this happened when I was there, I waited in the guard house, which was made of thick cement. You have to take cover when bullets are ricocheting around.

The OCs are very grateful for the ministry that is taken into prison. They say, "It makes our work easier, prisoners are changed to settle down, and trust God."

At the time of writing there is a white Italian man in prison. He has been convicted for five years. He is unable to eat the food, so I am taking in all that he is asking for every week.

An Open Door

I was privileged to be allowed into the prison, along with one or two of my fellow ministers. It took a long time to convince the guards that I was no threat, and that we had no ulterior motives for wanting to speak to the inmates.

The ministry that evolved was well worth the efforts it took to get it going. After a long time, the guards built up trust in us, as they saw the positive effect the gospel was having on those who were getting saved. They eventually even allowed us to start bringing some basic provisions for the inmates. God was giving us favour and His Kingdom was growing as a result.

Blessed are the Poor in Spirit

The prisoners were hungry for the good news, and grateful for the meagre offerings we would take in whenever we could. Often, they had been deserted by friends and family, and had lost the few worldly possessions they once owned. With no-one and nothing waiting for them outside, even if they ever were to be released, many were bitter, angry, depressed, and broken in spirit.

Asking nothing in return, we bring them news of the kindest, greatest, and most faithful companion man can have, the Forgiving God. The God who wanted to meet them, make them clean and new, and to give them the most priceless treasure any human can possess. Salvation. All without cost. All without condition or need to earn it.

We have also done what we could to show God's love and our genuine concern by providing basic practical necessities. Things like paracetamol for fevers, ailments and pain that otherwise would be left untreated, bottles of clean water during droughts, when there is no access to any water in the prison, occasionally a fresh change of clothes, soap and so on.

The Fields are Ripe unto Harvest

In 1990 I was permitted to go into Kamuli prison and preach. I think it was the first time that the prisoners heard the Gospel. At first when I was in Kamuli, I asked my friend, the Resident District Commissioner, for permission to pray with the prisoners there. He agreed.

The first day I went to prison there were about 60 men, and a few women who were ushered into the courtyard. I was told you have 20 minutes to talk. I was used to talking for an hour and a half, but I managed, speaking about Jesus being crucified with two criminals.

One scoffed, "If you are the Son of God, get us down off these crosses."

The other said, "Be quiet. This man has done nothing wrong, but we deserve to die." Then he said to Jesus, "Jesus, remember me when you come into your kingdom."

Jesus answered, "Today you will be with me in Paradise."

These two criminals represent the people in the world. There are those who cry out to God when they are in deep trouble, and want Him to deliver them, although they will continue in in their own wicked ways after deliverance. Then there are those who recognise their own guilt, and sin, and cry out for mercy. Jesus will never turn them away. They will be saved, and live forever with Him.

Then I asked the prisoners, "Which of the two are you?"

I think nearly all of the prisoners received salvation that day, surrendering their hearts and lives to the living Lord Jesus. It was wonderful. Being a prisoner in Uganda is on a par with being a slave, but those who have received Jesus are as free as a bird in their spirit!

I and Paster Okumu were the first born-again Christians to enter that prison. These days I make a visit to prison in Malukhu, in Mbale, every week, to preach the good news, and every week for the past 28 years prisoners have found Jesus there.

Week after week, month after month, year after year, we visit the prison. It was the darkest of places to begin with, but soon, behind those bars shone some of the Kingdom's brightest lights. Those who received Jesus, and those who started to listen to the bible teachings, underwent dramatic changes.

Some of the most hardened, coldest of criminals began to care about and even to pray for fellow inmates. Sour faces often turned to smiles, and heavy hearts rose with new life and renewed hope. The warmth of God's love and the power of his Word, bringing dead souls to life.

Many have been healed by the Holy Spirit's power. Many have been discipled over the years, and have been released to become pastors, apostles, evangelists, teachers, and prophets. They are changed forever.

Once you have met Jesus you are never the same again.

Improved Conditions

Conditions in prison were terrible in those days. There is a great improvement today, but prison is not at all like western countries. The sick bay has been given decent beds with hospital mattresses, and drugs are available, although some have to be bought.

The prison food has not improved, but the prisoners are now issued good quality, bright yellow uniforms, and are each given a small blanket.

Prisoners were also punished severely for any misbehaviour, whereas now, human rights have changed that. Their cases are also more likely to be heard than previously. They are no longer beaten, and the human rights people visit from time to time to keep an eye on things.

Inmates may be able to study and pass for P7, O level. There is a carpentry workshop. Some crafts are taught. They may even have a small radio.

Still Going Strong

The ministry to prison stopped only during COVID 19, because everyone had no choice by law but to isolate. But, except for that period of restrictions, I am blessed to have ministered in the prison here every week for the last 33 years.

It is often the case in many ministries, that the seeds of the gospel are sown but the preacher moves on before the fruits have time to appear. However, I have had the privilege of seeing the long-term effects of Jesus' saving power in many people's lives. That is because I find myself in situations where I can evangelise and also minister on a regular basis, especially when it comes to those who receive Jesus in the prison.

I meet ex-prisoners nearly every day in town. Many of them have grown so much in their faith and in the Word of God that they have become pastors, some even now hold high positions in the church. One pastor is ministering in Dubai! Lovely fruit!

More Testimonies

You have read Fred Mukhama's testimony, here are some more testimonies relating to the prison ministry.

Prison to Pulpit

There was a young man imprisoned for a few years, and he found Jesus there. On his release he went to his home in the village, and found the houses, and his family were no longer there. The whole family had died, but before they passed away they used all the money they had for drinking the local alcoholic brew, and had even sold their land to pay for their drink. He was devastated.

He went to a pastor near his home called Patrick. He lived in Busembatia. The pastor told Patrick to go into the church and fast and pray and said he would look after him.

After a short while, he came to Mbale, and told me what had happened. I prayed with him and, as far as I can recall, I gave him something, then the Red Cross also gave him a few necessities. He then returned back to the pastor in Busembatia.

Some years later he came to visit me. Some white people had visited Pastor Patrick's church and had paid for the ex-prisoner to go to Glad Tidings Bible School in Kampala. He married and became a pastor of a Full Gospel Church.

Healed from HIV

Another prisoner was very excited one day and asked to give his testimony. He had been diagnosed as HIV positive before entering prison. All prisoners have to be tested, and he found miraculously that he been healed.

Now he was HIV negative! He was jumping for joy. Praise the LIVING LORD JESUS.

A Wonderful Recovery

A prisoner collapsed during the service in prison, and some prisoners carried him out to the Sick Bay. I rushed to the Sick Bay as soon as the meeting finished and found the prisoner crying out to Jesus, almost totally gone. I prayed passionately in tongues, desperately praying that he would not die. Something happened and he started to regain his life, and he came through.

I discovered that he had just begun to take ARVs for AIDS, without taking breakfast. These drugs are so strong that he almost died. I sent in milk for him and he recovered and became strong. Then I began sending millet flour and sugar to prison every month to help those patients who were taking ARVs. This is on-going.

Love Provides

There was a Cholera outbreak some years back. No visitors were allowed in prison. The OC Prison requested me to help with JIK (Chlorine), rubber gloves, and brushes for cleaning. I took everything that was needed, entering the prison myself. If I remember correctly, no lives were lost.

Strength to Forgive

One day a prisoner stood up during the service, and announced that he had done something really bad to me, but I did not know him, and please would I forgive him? I said that of course I would forgive him, though I had no idea what crime he had committed. It was perhaps a year later when I was taking a short rest in town, sitting on a bench outside of a shop, when a man came up to me.

"Sister Christine! You're still alive! I have been praying every day that I would meet you again. Do you remember the prisoner that asked for your forgiveness in prison?"

"Oh yes," I said.

"This is a miracle, an answer to my prayers." He knelt down, and said, "I was the man that was riding the bodaboda bicycle when you asked me to carry your heavy bag to church in Namatala. Will you forgive me?"

I remembered, and my heart hardened.

That Sunday I was going to church, but for some reason that I cannot recall, I was carrying three huge study Bibles. These were my favourite books. I was always delving into them, and God spoke to me through them. They were heavy, so I called a bodaboda bicycle to carry the bag as I walked alongside it. As I reached the top of the incline, I saw a very beautiful cow and stopped to admire it. When I turned around, the bodaboda was gone with the books, my phone, my bank card, and my money! I was absolutely devastated. I reached the church in a state of near collapse, but still managed to preach. Afterwards, attempts were made to try and find the bibles, even over the radio. They were unique in Uganda. People prayed. They were never found BUT this thief could not rest until he had found me and confessed. After the hardening of heart, I, by setting my will, made the decision to forgive him. A weight fell from me, and the thief almost danced for joy.

It was not easy!

Encouragement

When I was walking home from prison some years back, I found a man sitting on the grass verge along the main road.

"Sister Christine! Do you remember me? I was in prison, and you preached to me."

I rarely remember prisoners after release. The prison uniform makes it hard to distinguish someone in plain clothes. I was very disappointed in him. He was clearly drunk, and I felt my work in prison was having no effect whatsoever. However, a few yards down the road another man, wheeling a bicycle, hailed me.

"Sister Christine, do you remember me? I was in prison, and you prayed for me and I got saved."

"Are you going to church?" I asked.

"Yes, I go to Deliverance Church, I am married, and have a family. I have a job. All is well."

My spirits lifted. God was showing me never to give up. At least about half of the prisoners are truly saved, even if the other half may not be.

"Just keep on discipling them and praying with them. It is not your job to save them, my gal!"

Chapter 12

Radio Outreach

One of the more recent ways we have found to reach people, both with the gospel, and with solid biblical teaching, is through radio broadcasting. The sessions are not cheap, and limited funds have curbed our plans, on more than one occasion, for more regular sessions. This has stopped us altogether from recording some weeks, but we keep coming back to use this media whenever we are able to afford it. Our ability to use the radio to preach and teach every week is affected not only by the station's fees, but also problems with transport.

The reason we invest in doing the radio program is because there have been times when this ministry has appeared to bring as much, if not even more, fruit than localised meetings, seminars and so on.

The preaching of the gospel message and teaching broadcasts, usually presented by me, a local minister or occasionally a guest speaker, reach far and wide through our weekly radio program. Many Christians, who are unable to attend church, or who attend a church with poor quality teaching, tune in weekly, keen to hear more of the Word.

Carrying On Through COVID

During the COVID crisis, there were times we were able to go to the station to record the broadcasts, and even when that was not allowed, we found a way to record them from home and have them taken to be broadcast from the station. Because of this, although Church meetings were cancelled, many people still had access to the gospel and the teaching of the Word of God for much of the outbreak/lockdown time.

New Believers, and Converts from Other Faiths

Not only believers, but also those of other faiths, Muslims etc., and Atheists alike, often say they find themselves drawn to listen. Some who get saved call the station to let us know. We can't always respond to every message, as there just isn't enough time, but it is always an encouragement to hear what God is doing through the broadcasts.

It isn't always easy for those who turn to Christ, especially Muslim women, who are often then thrown out with their children and left to fend for themselves. We hear also from some of the Muslim men who convert to Jesus, and who likewise find themselves ostracised by their family and their community. Some are even threatened with their lives.

Though we are limited in what we can do, it is a comfort to know that whatever people must suffer for believing in Jesus in this life, they will be secure and safe for all eternity, and will reap a reward in

Heaven. Not one soul will ever be the worse off for having accepted Christ as their Lord and Saviour.

I, and the occasional guest speaker, always encourage new converts to attend local churches to get fellowship and teaching, and any other support they need from the leadership and congregation there. We have to do this, as we are always dreadfully limited, financially and practically, and already facing more needs than we can meet in our own churches and communities.

Testimonies

People of all ages and backgrounds also call in with testimonies of healing miracles, relationship transformations, family rifts being mended, deliverance taking place, and more. Others call in to thank us, or with questions - hungry for more of the truth of God's word. These broadcasts are a wonderful tool I have been blessed to make use of, and I intend to continue using while ever I am able.

I can only hope that by sharing with you how important the good news of Jesus is, and how important it is to spread the good news whenever we can, that you will be challenged to accept Jesus as your own personal saviour today. If you already know Jesus as your Lord, I want to encourage you to make the most of every opportunity you are given, to share Jesus in your own daily life too.

Chapter 13

Education and Sponsorships

Education is greatly valued in Uganda, and parents have both government and private schools to choose from.

Government schools are supposed to be free, but they are not. Fees must be paid every term, uniforms and books must be bought, and (compulsory) extra-curriculum activities also have to be paid for. Government schools are slightly cheaper to attend than private ones, but they have more than 100 students in each class.

Government teachers are paid a fairly reasonable salary, but it is not enough. Often, they have to take on additional work in private schools, and move around, teaching in different places every day.

Competition

All the schools vie with each other to achieve the highest exam pass rate, wanting recognition, so that parents will prefer to send their children there.

Both private and government schools alike take this 'competition' very seriously. Bright students are given extra lessons. In boarding schools, the children are woken at three in the morning for their studies. Day students go to school from 8am until 5 or 6pm, and some even attend on Saturdays and Sundays!

A Hard Life for Children

I am so sorry for the children who have to walk long distances to school. They pass my house as soon as it is light. That is 6am. Then, I see them walking home at 6 or 7pm. Food is often not a priority, and they will probably not have had any breakfast. When they arrive home, they have to wash their uniforms for the next day, bathe, eat, sleep and rise at 5am to prepare to walk to school again. Standards are extremely low, as you may imagine.

Not all children go to school. There may not be enough money for boys to complete their education, and some girls are left (they are kept at home), as marriage fodder!

A father may ask a man for an enormous amount of money to marry his daughter. There is a girl near me in the village, who has been left.

Employment Opportunities

I have a really good boy here, who works with the donkeys for me on Sundays. His name is Moses. He is about 16/17, and he lives with his other siblings and his grandmother. I wept when he told me what happened to him.

He lived in another area with his mother and father, and one day his father took him, and some siblings, in a taxi to Namabasa. He left them with their aunty, and later they were shifted to the grandmother. Why? He had found another woman who didn't want the children. I felt Moses' pain at being rejected and sent away. Sometimes the father sends school fees, but other times he doesn't. This is a common occurrence here.

I employ another boy about the same age, to cut grass for the donkeys, and to help generally when it is needed. He seems to be a good boy too. He lives with his grandmother; they sleep on a mat together. They had no mosquito net until I gave them an old one. They were struggling to find enough to eat. Now he receives 170,000UGX a month, that's about £35 (GBP). I see him wearing good clothes now, and they are both eating regularly.

A few days after he first came to work for me, he became seriously sick with malaria. He lay on a mattress in my sitting room, where I had to treat him with intravenous drips. It was then I gave him the mosquito net. At Christmas I sent him home with rice, sugar, cooking oil, bread, and extra money. His grandmother was so happy with me.

A Disappointment

A few of our visitors have sponsored the education of some of the children of my workers. Sadly, I found the results were often less than honouring to the sponsors. One girl became pregnant and quit school, but she, her mother, and the father of the child. hid it and continued to lie to me about her welfare.

Her sponsor was sending the school fees, while she stayed out of school and was having a baby! After her baby was born, the girl was sent back for her further education course. It was more than a year before I found out the truth, and then had to inform the sponsor, who, like me, was so disappointed. He wanted to give up any further educational sponsorship.

Battling Corruption

Another boy, who was exceptionally clever, lived in my home for some time when he was studying. He qualified up to Diploma level, and he was going to be accepted by World Vision in Karamoja. They wanted him to drive, so I sent him to driving school.

Then the officer who was handling these recruits told him, "The job is yours, after you give me a million shillings!"

I was so angry that I told the boy to leave and come back to Mbale. I wanted to report that man, but the Lord would not allow me to. I sent the young man to look for work elsewhere, but he never found another job. He stayed at home, impregnated a girl, and began to drink. His life was ruined. He had to stay with the girl, who he never really loved. Later, thankfully, he found a job as a night watchman with a charity called Jenga.

Some Success Stories

Another boy was sent to train as a nurse. He did his best and he qualified, and I was more than happy with him.

Two orphan siblings, a girl and a boy, also came to my home for some time. Their mother had attended our church but became terribly sick and died. I took the body to their village with Marion, who was with me at that time.

The girl stayed in my home whist she trained to become a teacher. She finished well and found a good job with Child of Hope. After that, she went on to get married and have children.

Her brother also stayed with us at home, but he was badly behaved. Nevertheless, he trained in catering.

Two more girls were sponsored for nursing. One sadly became pregnant and left the school, but the other qualified and is now working.

Resigned Reluctance

Overall, despite the success stories and the kindness of the sponsors involved, I have been greatly disappointed with sponsorships. I would never handle another one, unless perhaps it was only up to P7 level.

I would hate to send anyone to university, because they are well and truly spoiled there -

drinking, drugs, partying, sleeping around, and becoming proud! May God have mercy on the education system in Uganda!

Chapter 14

Animal Welfare

I may not have come to Uganda to help animals, but I soon discovered there was a distinct lack of care for the wellbeing of many of the animals that I saw. There were a lot of strays, some abandoned, and some born without a home.

Even the farm animals were fortunate if they had caring owners. I often saw signs of disease and neglect when I passed by properties where they were fortunate enough to afford to keep livestock of any kind.

There were some sick, and neglected animals that I just could not leave to suffer. I helped the owners to put matters right if they were willing. When all else failed, I took the animal. Before long, I was taking in not only sick and abandoned livestock, but also unwanted pets. Thankfully, a lot of them recovered and became wonderful companions to me and others, who offered to re-house them when they were well enough.

I have had sick turkeys stray onto my property, and a lame cow gifted to me, which we nursed back to health, and which repaid us in milk and calves for years to come. Some of the dogs I took in stayed with me and provided security, protecting myself and both the property and livestock as well. I ended up with donkeys which paid for their keep by carrying goods and people all over the place.

There were of course, occasions where I had no choice but to have some of the animals put to sleep. As heartbreaking as those times were, the recovery stories made it all worthwhile in the end.

One of the practices I saw that really disturbed me was the way locals would carry dozens of live chickens, all dangling precariously from bikes and other vehicles. It was inhumane and animals suffered terribly because of this crude method of transportation. I complained to the officials about it, and I even paid for the police to be on the lookout for these chicken transporters, to put a stop to what they were doing.

It proved to be very effective, as after a while I saw this method of transporting animals happen less frequently and can only put it down to the efforts of the police to stamp the practice out. I thank God, though it seems a small victory in the face of such abundant general ignorance about animal welfare here.

Some onlookers are offended that I take the time to look after animals, when the needs of people here are so great. I can understand why they feel this way, but at the same time I cannot ignore the plight of any of God's living creatures. Besides which, in my opinion, the companionship, unconditional love, and even practical help - by way of protection, creation of jobs, milk, eggs, the sale of offspring, their ability to transport people and goods, etc. that we receive in return, often far outweighs the care they have received from us in the beginning.

Does God not say that a righteous man takes good care of his animals? (Proverbs 12:10). Does He not also even encourage us to give to those who can offer nothing in return? (Luke 14:14) If God says that the cattle on a thousand hills belong to Him (Psalm 50:10), and that He takes note of every sparrow that falls to the ground (Matthew 10:29), is it not fit for His children to see the plight of His creation and be moved with compassion for them? Well, I believe it certainly is.

I am not alone in my views thankfully. There are like-minded people who often contribute to the welfare of the animals in my care. Such people as the vet who helped look after some of my cows, a fellow missionary who took in some needy puppies, a pastor friend who has agreed to take the animals when I cannot them keep any longer, and friends abroad who have sent funds, donated flea treatments, harnesses, and all kinds of other useful, helpful things. I am so grateful to them, and to the Lord from whom all blessings flow.

It's a Dog's Life!

More than any other type of animal, it is the abandoned and abused dogs that seem to find their way to me, one way or another. We, that is to say

William, Matthew, Julius, and myself, have all loved and cared for many such dogs over the years. Here are a few that spring to mind as I write…

Bambi

Whilst living in Busamaga, I opened the kitchen door one morning to find a small animal curled up in a corner. It was a puppy! It was male, completely hairless, and his skin was hot and burning.

When I realised it was a dog, I exclaimed, "Oohh bambi!" In Luganda, 'bambi' means 'sorry.'

Bambi was taken into care and treated for mange, and, as his hair started to grow back, we discovered he was black and brown. He had beautiful eyes that pierced into your soul.

Bambi has been with us for about 10 years now. He was taken away for about six months when I was severely ill, almost at the point of death. The person promised to take care of him for me, but instead he was treated badly, and had lost about two thirds of his weight by the time he was returned. He had already suffered more than enough!

Bobby

About 10 years ago, a man was walking past our house carrying a cardboard box. My worker, Lomongin, shouted out to him in a great big voice, "Oi!"

The man threw the box and quickly ran away. In the box we found a beautiful but very frighted and aggressive puppy, soon after to be known as Bobby. It was a tough little thing, so much so that we were all afraid of it, and no one managed to pick it out of the box. We decided to leave it in the box, in hopes that it might calm down a little.

Later that night, Julius was keeping watch in the compound, when he decided that even if the puppy bit him, he would remove it from the box. Wearing a thick jacket, he picked the puppy out of the box and held it tightly to his chest, until at last it relaxed. Julius had won the dog's trust, and by the morning we found a sweet animal awaiting us, who was readily taking milk and food.

Bobby is a big, long-bodied dog, who is gentle and sweet natured - a real gentleman! He is beautiful, with long fine hair, his top-coat black and the under-coat is brown. He has a long, pointed nose, and looks like the famous dog Lassie, if you know that story.

He was also taken away by someone else when I was sick, but thankfully he was well taken are of, and so never suffered as Bambi did.

Lady and Mishi

When a lady called Emma Stewart was living in my house with me, about 10 years ago, she went for a break to Mto Moyoni, a Christian Retreat Centre in Jinja. She returned home with a very small washing up bowl. Inside were two puppies.

Three puppies had been left outside the gate at Mto Moyoni, all extremely sick with Parvo (a killer disease that puppies catch). Dr Herbert, a good vet, treated them, but sadly one died. The remaining pups recovered and were brought to me.

They have both grown into strong, big, healthy dogs. Lady, who is all brown with short hair, is by far the biggest. Muscular, and powerful!

Her sister Mishi is not quite as large, and is black with a bit of brown, and her head is patterned with a white stripe down the nose. She always demands to be petted, 24 hours a day, if at all possible.

They once caught and killed a monkey in a Eucalyptus plantation near my home, here in Namabasa. Monkeys come and go from time to time, in the plantation, and all the dogs love it. The chase is on when the monkeys arrive, but thanks be to God, they have never been able to catch any more.

Simba

In 2021, Simba, who was living with some other homeless dogs, was found under a parked car outside the Central Police station in Mbale. He is brown in colour, and about the size of a Labrador, but back then, he was all skin and bone. We thought he must be a pup or a young dog.

My friend Faye found him and immediately put him into the care of a vet, who, it later transpired, knew nothing about keeping a dog. The vet was unable to look after Simba, who somehow or other ended up in my care.

He started to bleed, and upon inspection, our good vet Dr Levi found a tumour and so operated on him to remove it. It was a sexually transmitted disease. We knew then that Simba was obviously more than a pup. He was castrated, and another problem around his teats was also cleaned and stitched.

Even now he cries each time food is given to him. He eats extremely quickly, as though he thinks that he may never have another meal in his life.

Simba is quite a simple dog and a very slow learner. I think he was starved for such a long time it may have affected his brain. He constantly demands attention, and literally cries to be petted. He has become quite fat, but still he begs for more food. He is a sweet dog and is so needy. We want to make sure that he never has to go hungry or uncared for ever again.

Chelee (I call her Chelsea)

She is brown and thin. To this day I have never seen such a thin dog. She was a walking skeleton, with teats hanging almost to the ground. She had six puppies. I found her when walking to church near the sewage ponds. Someone was keeping her in a sort of tent made of cardboard boxes and bits of corrugated iron.

It was a struggle to have that dog removed from her owner, but somehow we managed to rescue her and three of her puppies. The others were stolen before we could remove them, and the likelihood is that they probably never survived. The three we rescued had Parvo, and one of those died, even with treatment. The remaining two grew well, and we found a good home for them.

In 2021, Chelsea survived a fight with our other dog, Lady. Lady is big, Chelsea much smaller. Lady bit right through a blood vessel, and Chelsea was bleeding to death. Blood was everywhere.

Matthew caught her, and we pressed a clean cloth into the wound and stopped the bleeding. Dr Levi came and cleaned and stitched her up. She was given a drip and survived. Strangely, she likes to be with Lady!

We all love her. She is nervous and highly strung, but at night she relaxes and sleeps with her arms around a young dog called Veronica. They love each other and lick each other.

Bonnie and his sisters

I think it was in 2022, that a young Muslim boy brought us four puppies that had not been weaned. Their mother had been frightened in a thunderstorm and had run away, leaving her puppies. They were starving. The boy could not handle the situation, and his father refused to have anything to do with the puppies.

We bottle-fed them, and all survived. A good home was found for all except Bonnie, who we kept. He is a tall thin dog, dark in colour, and very similar to a greyhound.

Angie, William and Veronica

My friend Faye, who is working with the street dogs, brought Angie with her six puppies in 2022.

Angie is a small black dog who is sweet natured. Her pups were delivered on the street outside the police station. They started moving around and were in danger of being run over on the busy main road. Faye was crying, and although I was quite reluctant, I found that I had to take them. Angie had four huge black puppies, and two tiny brown puppies, and all but one were female.

We found homes for four of them, leaving us with a big black one we call William, and a small brown one we call Veronica. Unfortunately, we heard that two of the beautiful black puppies we gave out have come to sad demise. One died because treatment was delayed for tic fever, and another went missing. We believe it was stolen.

Stanley

Stanley was thrown through the gate as a young puppy, in 2022. He is a local breed. He is brown with huge upright ears and is rather naughty. He picks anything and everything that may be hanging off the edge of the table.

If you speak harshly to him, he tends to become aggressive. However, if you speak nicely, he is very obedient, and responds well. He is a lovely boy.

Feeding the Multitude

It is expensive keeping the dogs, but the cost is not as bad as in the UK. Basic diet is pounded silver fish mixed with maize flour and a little fine maize brand. This is cooked together, and they like it with soup of silver fish. From time to time, we are able to buy supplements – sheep heads, chicken feet, chicken livers, pork, head of a pig, and when available, the head or leg of a camel. The cheapest meat is lungs of cow, and they have that sometimes. We buy these extras when we have money; otherwise, it is basic silver fish.

Breaking the Chain

We all love Bobby, Lady, Mishi, Simba, Chelee, Bonnie, Angie, Stanley, and all the others, and want them to be loved and cared for, and to live good, long lives here with us. We had more dogs before the ones I have mentioned, but they grew old, and died. It is sad when any animal ends its allotted time here on earth, but it is a blessing to know that we have been able to love and care for so many of them until the very end.

As much as we love the puppies, it is important that we break the cycle of unwanted pets, so all the dogs we have rescued have been 'fixed' - that is to say, they can no longer reproduce.

Paying for this service is worth it, to ensure no 'accidental' breeding among animals in our care, or in the care of anyone who takes them to keep as pets.

Chapter 15

Faithful Friends

It is impossible to list all of the amazing people I have encountered, or had the privilege of working alongside, over the last 33 years in Uganda. But, let me tell you about a few of the ones who have laboured with me faithfully, their stories of sorrow, of miracles, of tears, and of joy.

The Pastor at Kabale

During the first years in Uganda, I went to Kabale with Pastor Okumu. We were welcomed by a 'born again' church, and I ministered in discipleship. While we were there, the Pastor's wife died after giving birth. The baby died as well. This was the time that AIDS was rampant, and people were ignorant and in denial.

When we were planning to go back, the Pastor asked me to stay on and lead the church for him, as he was weak and grieving over his wife. He wanted to go back to his home in Fort Portal for a while. I agreed, and we planned to meet in one month's time in Fort Portal, where I would break my journey on the way back to Kamuli.

I had a wonderful time with the church, teaching them about praise, worship, marriage, discipleship, Holy Spirit baptism, gifts of the Spirit, and more. They soaked up the teachings like sponges and began moving in the Spirit. I had a counselling day, and many who came were delivered. They really loved me.

One day the whole church went for a picnic to Lake Bunyoni. It meant climbing up near-vertical hills. I was younger then! It was beautiful. I went for a short boat trip in a dug-out tree which we had to paddle, and not move around in, for fear of the boat overturning. The lake was so calm, and incredibly beautiful. A day that I will remember always.

Finally, it was time to leave. I caught the bus and travelled over hills and down valleys of the most glorious landscape. Early morning mist made the tops of the hills appear to be islands floating in the clouds. On reaching Fort Portal, there wasn't anyone there to meet the bus. I was in a strange place and had no contacts there. Those were the days before mobile phones and internet! I inquired after the name of the Pastor, but no-one knew him.

I found there was a Church of Uganda Guest house, and a caring lady escorted me, carrying my heavy case on her head and my guitar in her hand. I booked in, and enquiries were made for the Pastor, and he was found.

He was terribly sick but made a tremendous effort to get up and see me. I was shocked to see the state he was in and spent the whole day with him. He certainly was not able to go back to the church, and neither was I. I was expected back in Kamuli.

I had to leave the next day, and shortly after, the Pastor died. It was a classic case of AIDS. I felt bad about leaving the church, but it went on to do well, and a new Pastor grew up into the position and took over. About twenty years later he and his wife found me in Mbale, and we had a wonderful reunion. Now he has an international ministry.

Simon and Margaret

My night watchman, Simon, and his wife were the most zealous worshippers in my home. They were living in abject poverty with several children to care for, and the wages I paid were nowhere near what was needed to keep that family. When we left Busamaga later, we went with our faithful night watchman.

We had only been back in the area a short while when, one Sunday evening, just before Simon was due to come on night duty, he had a serious asthma attack and died. It was terrible for his wife, Margaret, and all their (I think there were six) children. They would all have been looking to me to help them in their distress, but at that time I had absolutely nothing that I could give them. I sent my condolences but stayed away, knowing that no-one would ever believe that a Muzungu was broke.

I heard that some relatives of Simon had turned up with big vehicles. They came to transport the body to Soroti, along with the widow and children. It was such a relief for me not to have to carry the guilt of being unable to provide the financial and practical help they all so badly needed. Some of the children stayed in the care of the relatives, while Margaret returned home with just three of them.

I went to visit them in their old home; one mud-walled room, with a mud floor and an iron-sheet roof. I shared Margaret's predicament in my newsletter, and kind people donated enough money to build her a new, permanent house in Namabasa. She still had struggles, but at least she and the children had a proper place to call home.

Steve Jesney

A missionary, Steve, our faithful brother and friend, joined us regularly for prayer. He was a builder by trade and made a great big wooden cross for me to put outside my home. It was a signal to all the evil powers in Busamaga to stay away.

As he was nailing the Cross piece into place he came into the house, sat down, and started to weep.

He said, "As I was hammering the nails, I felt that I was nailing Jesus to the Cross!"

There is power in the Cross of Christ!

When I left that place, I took the cross, and laid it in my compound. From there it slowly disappeared into the soil, as termites worked on it.

Steve sadly passed away due to a brain tumour, and will always be sadly missed by myself, and all those who knew and loved him. Thankfully I know our goodbyes are just temporary, as all of us who love Christ can look forward to a glorious heavenly reunion!

Maria and her Children

Maria had two small children, and no husband (another abandoned woman among the majority in Africa). Her son was called Lomongin, and her daughter was Nashaka. Maria always dressed Nashaka in long dresses, but one day Nashaka tripped, and I saw her legs were bowed and severely misshapen.

A new children's hospital called CURE had just opened in Mbale, specialising in orthopaedics, and operating on babies born with large heads. I spoke to Maria about it, and she agreed to take Nashaka there.

Nashaka was not so easily convinced and fought the doctor with all her Karamojong warrior ancestry. With a great deal of loving care, she was persuaded to undergo an operation. It was a complete success, and even when she turned 18 years of age, her legs were still perfectly straight. She had been studying for her O-levels from her home in the slums. A sponsor came to her aid, and she went to boarding school - a miraculous blessing for her.

Nashaka's brother, Lomongin, was a boy that demonstrated over-friendliness. He always threw himself over visitors and wanted to help them desperately. He had a needy spirit.

Someone sponsored him in school for 7 years, but he was a slow learner and he failed completely. Upon finishing Primary, Lomongin was awarded a P7 certificate declaring him to be a failure. When I tested him, I found that he was not able to read or write, he did not know numbers well, and he was unable to distinguish between the denominations in money.

I also noticed that his head was small and a little misshapen, and my conclusion was that Maria had been unable to feed herself or provide milk for, and to feed, her children sufficiently. Nashaka suffered with rickets, and Lomongin became a slow learner.

Knowing Lomongin would have little chance of employment, I decided to take him on to help with the animals in the compound. He was beyond happy to have a job, and to earn money.

Maria's Battle with AIDS

Maria later became sick. I suspected AIDS, so took her for testing. She tested positive and was immediately given drugs. After a while, she became strong. Then a friend persuaded her to fast and pray for three days, without drugs, so that God would heal her. Sadly, within just a short while, Maria died.

That was presuming on God - someone presumed this was what God wanted, but they were wrong. It is almost always advisable to take the practical help that is offered to us by medical professionals, as so often God provides for us in this way. We should wait for God to make His will clear to us personally before we refuse the help offered and, instead, decide to take what may well be totally unnecessary risks. Unfortunately, it is not uncommon for people here to die from AIDS, after presuming God had wanted them to stop taking the medicine to prove they had 'faith.'

This does not mean that God cannot, or will not, ever do a miracle that doesn't involve doctors, medicine, practical or financial help from other people. I have personally known a few people be miraculously healed of AIDS. A perfect example is that of my housekeeper, who was on AIDS drugs for 15 years, when suddenly God healed her. After her usual testing, it was found she was negative. What a testimony to glorify the Lord! Her evidence was from the hospital - the lab reports before and after. To God be the glory.

Maria's Miracle Cow

I received a cow as a gift from a brother in the UK, through a Pastor from the Dokolo Lira District. It arrived in Namatala, along with other gifts to the church. The cow had been thrown off a lorry and was injured. She was a brown beauty, with long horns and a gorgeous hump.

The cow was unable to stand, so Maria (the poor sister who later died of AIDS), cut grass and fed it to her every day. The LC1's son also came to turn the cow every day, by yanking her over with her tail. After three weeks, the end of the tail came off! It was thought that she had some disease that caused this, but I still wonder whether that was a tale conjured up to alleviate my feelings.

The local drunkards, sipping their homemade brew with long straws out of a communal pot, prophesied that the cow would die. And, after three weeks of little improvement, I resigned myself to the inevitable and called the butcher.

As he was on his way, coming to slaughter the animal, she stood up!

Our miracle cow, who we named Maria, (after her carer), fully recovered, but then sadly miscarried the calf she was carrying. She went on, however, to produce a healthy calf every year after that for more than 20 years. A lot of poor brethren at the church benefited from being given one of her calves. She was known by everyone in the slums of Namatala, and instantly recognised by her broken-off tail.

Maria (the cow) was loved so greatly that when the time came that she was not able to walk anymore, I called the vets to have her euthanised, rather than have her slaughtered by the butcher. The neighbours were horrified, saying that I had poisoned the meat. My dear friend was given an honourable burial in the corner of the compound, much to the disgust of disapproving onlookers.

Julius

I hired a pastor, Julius, as a manager. His job was to supervise all of the day-to-day work in my home and compound, where a few workers looked after the animals, birds, and garden. He handled everything including all the money, except the wages. It was extremely difficult for me to find faithful, trustworthy people in Uganda, so Julius was a special gift from God. He was close to me and shared in my spiritual life as well, considering me to be his mentor.

I first met Julius in prison, where he received the Lord Jesus Christ as his Saviour. He asked me for a Bible, and I found an old one and gave it to him. He was on remand for six months, before being released with no case to answer.

Julius was married and had a son. Unfortunately, while he was in prison all his property had been sold, even his cow, which he loved. Soon after his release, he came to me begging for a job. He had qualifications up to A-level, an impressive and rare achievement in Uganda.

"I have no job for someone of your level of education, I need a herdsman," I had told him.

As he was leaving, he turned around and said, "I'll take it!"

So, Julius started working with some of the animals I placed in his care - about six oxen. They responded wonderfully well to him. When he walked, they walked. When he stopped, they stopped, all with their eyes on him, waiting for the signal to walk on. I was greatly impressed, especially as Ugandans are not known for their love for animals.

It is not easy to adjust to 'normal' life after being in prison, and it was good for Julius to work with the animals. It relaxed his mind. Slowly, I felt he was ready for more responsibility, and so I sent him to Kampala on various jobs, like buying me an air ticket - a great test which he passed with honours. He soon became my right-hand man.

God gave Julius the Gift of Healing. His church was situated within a Muslim stronghold, yet in the first year the converts grew to about 200, mostly Muslim women, who had received all kinds of supernatural healings.

Barren women conceived. There were difficult pregnancies, where women who were waiting for caesarean sections gave birth even before reaching the operating theatre. Some people called for him at the point of death, and they recovered after prayer. Sometimes, the relatives were already planning the burial!

It was a beautiful ministry.

Chapter 16

God is Real, Religion without Him is Dead.

Here are a few more occasions when I saw the Lord at work in my life.

I was at a ladies' intercessory prayer meeting years ago, and we had a visitor from the USA. He wanted to pray for me. I put my hands together in prayer, and he sat opposite me and put his hands over mine. They became the hands of Jesus to me! Always remember that Jesus is praying for you.

There was an elderly brother who sometimes came to my home, and we read the Bible together. He became extremely sick and was taken to the hospital. His wife refused to allow me to visit him. As I was resting on the sofa a voice shouted within me, "I was sick, and you never visited me." Jumping up, I put on my coat and went to the hospital. He was gravely ill.

I asked, "Would you like me to read the Bible to you?"

He told me that he would. After I read for a while, his wife came into the room. She was clearly angry that I was there, so I said my goodbyes and left. Later that night he died, and I was very grateful that I had taken the chance to visit him.

Recently I had an amazing experience. Feeling frustrated with a number of things happening in my home, I decided to walk down through the Eucalyptus plantation, over the rice fields to the church. I sat and talked to the Lord about everything.

Tired out, I fell asleep for a few minutes, then suddenly woke as I felt as if I was being lifted. Sitting up, I was astonished to find that I was covered in glittering dust! I looked up to see where it had fallen from, but there was nothing.

I said to myself, *What is it?*

I held my skirt up to collect the gold dust, and went to the door to call Pastor Osika.

"Can you see this, Pastor?"

"Yes," he said, "What is it?"

We sat together in church and wondered. All I knew was that I felt overwhelmingly happy about it, and up to today I am still very happy about it. I am a blessed woman. I am greatly loved, I am accepted in the Beloved… Thank you, Jesus.

I believe God hates religion. God wants a relationship, and He is looking for a friend and a lover. My desire has always been to find God; the real, living God. These experiences I have shared are written in my spirit and will never be forgotten. If you seek God with all of your heart, you will be found by him too. (Jeremiah 29:13)

I wanted you to know about some of the revelations I have had of Jesus. They are personal, and precious to me. Salvation is relationship, not a religion. Most importantly, I receive from the Holy

Spirit nearly every day, as I read the Bible. The Bible is alive to everyone who is filled with the Holy Spirit. Jesus is the Word made flesh. Take your Bible, and kiss it, as you kiss the Son. And never forget, Jesus says, "Love one another, AS I HAVE LOVED YOU."

Chapter 17

A Personal Resurrection

In mid-December 2020, I became very sick. I found myself in Joy Hospice, though I never remembered going there. Pastor Julius, Pastor Oscar, and Administrator Fred had carried me there.

Before this, I had become ill with a strange sickness. My vision was badly affected, and I had overdosed a bit on some medicine. I felt exhausted. When my eyes closed, I saw people, young and old, walking silently, slowly, and looking right at me. There were thousands of them! When I opened my eyes, everything was normal. When I closed them, there were the people again. Was I hallucinating? Was I in the place of the dead?

There were times I could not speak, yet could see, hear, and understand the people around me. I had a scan which showed I had not had a stroke. Was this demonic? I do not know! Who knows? (What I do know, is that Jesus has overcome the powers of death and hell. Hallelujah!)

After more clinical tests, the doctors found that I had a serious infection of the bladder, and that malaria had also developed. In the Hospice they put me in a room on my own - where people are taken when they are about to die. They had put a cannula on my hand, and I was on a drip. That night, my doctor came and looked in my eyes. It was deep unto deep.

"You are going to die… May I call your son in New Zealand?"

"Yes." I relaxed, and gave up.

I had peace in my heart. Our people here in Uganda began to make plans to take the body to the mortuary, but Julius was not prepared to allow death to swallow me. He was in deep prayer with others, including my son, Nic, in New Zealand.

All through the night the nurse was checking my blood pressure and oxygen and attending to my cannula. (I thought she was doing embroidery on my hand at times.) Then I heard my morning alarm. It was 7 o'clock. I had survived the night.

My health began to improve. I was being brought back to this world. After a few days I was discharged! Alive and well and blessed beyond measure.

Starting Again

There was still work for me to do, and there were problems that I had not finished solving in the ministry. When I was strong enough, I met with the Church leaders, and God moved among us. We opened up our hearts to each other, and God powerfully brought us together in unity. It was a miracle.

I felt like the contents of my mind had been totally washed away, and it was only slowly, over time, that I started to remember my former life. To me, it seemed as though God had given me a fresh start.

A Sad Homecoming

By Christmas I was back home, and a kind friend took me to a hotel for Christmas lunch. At my house however, all was quiet, there were no decorations and nothing special to mark the day. Just two cats remained at my home. All my dogs, donkeys, geese, and guinea fowls had been taken by an American lady who had wanted them, and was looking after them. It felt so empty without them. She only allowed me to have one dog back.

I tried to appreciate that it was a wonderful blessing that the lady was willing to take the animals when I was at deaths door, but coming back and finding most of them gone caused me much sorrow. I love all my animals dearly. (But God is good, and later it would happen that all my animals came back home to me, when the lady had returned to America.)

The Birthday I Didn't Expect to See

The following day, Boxing Day, was my birthday, and oh how I praised Jesus. I had reached 80 years! I thought I was going to miss it. Another friend took me for lunch on my birthday. God had given me the gift of another year of life to celebrate.

Back to Work

God is good. Now, several years after my miraculous recovery, I am still here in Uganda, in my beautiful home, surrounded by my lovely animals, and still ministering.

The radio ministry continues. Many have been saved through the broadcasts, and lives have been changed by the teaching it brings to people. All glory be to God on high. Likewise, the Prison ministry continues to reach lost souls and to help new believers to mature through regular fellowship, prayer, the preaching of the gospel, and teaching of the word.

My work as Overseer of God is Alive Churches is still ongoing. It has not been easy, but I have seen that God is with us, and His will is being done through the ministry. What more could I want?

I am humbled by the trust others have placed in me, and thankful to God that I am still able to carry out my responsibilities and to minister in such a variety of ways, all at the ripe old age of 83!

Epilogue

How do you know what is going to happen tomorrow? The length of our life is uncertain as the morning fog. Now you see it, and soon it is gone.

My life passes swiftly away, often filled with tragedy. My years disappear like swift ships, like the eagle that swoops upon its prey. We are here but for a moment, strangers in the land, as our fathers were before us. Our days on earth are like a shadow, gone so soon, without a trace.

Lord, help me to realise how brief my time on earth will be. Help me to know that I am here but for a moment more.

The world is fading away. But whoever keeps doing the will of God will live forever. (1 John 2:17)

They will grow old like worn out clothing, and you will change them like a man putting on a new shirt and throwing away the old one. But You Yourself never grow old, You are forever, and Your years never end. (Hebrews 1:11)

Jesus Christ is the same yesterday, today, and forever.

(Hebrews 13:8)

AMEN!

An Important Question in Closing

Having read this book dear Reader, I should like to ask you a question. Where will YOU go when you die? Are you sure that you have received salvation?

If you say, "I am a Catholic, Muslim, Charismatic (or whatever)." you are not saved merely because you have joined a church - your religion is unable to take you to Heaven.

If you say, "I have been baptised," your baptism will not take you to Heaven.

If you say, "I have built schools, orphanages, hospitals etc." you are not going to Heaven no matter what you have done. Good works without salvation will not take you to Heaven.

If you say, "I am a good person," you have deceived yourself and make the Bible out to be a liar, for it says that ALL HAVE SINNED, AND FALLEN SHORT OF GOD'S GLORY.

Have you ever told a lie?

Have you ever looked with lust after a woman?

Have you ever been angry?

Have ever been jealous or wanted what other people have?

Have you ever said I am better than others? This is the sin of pride and of self-righteousness.

There is no-one who has not sinned. Because of this SIN, no-one may enter the Holy place where the Holy God dwells. God made a way for ALL who have sinned to enter His Heaven to live with Him for ever.

Today will you allow me to show you the way to enter?

It is through the Blood shed by the Lord Jesus Christ on the Cross that our sins are forgiven. There is no remission of sin without the shedding of blood. Only the pure, spotless, sinless Blood of Christ Himself can remove all sin. Do you believe this?

The steps to salvation are simple:

1st step - Acknowledge that you have sinned.

2nd step - Ask God for forgiveness through the Blood of Jesus.

3rd step - Receive your forgiveness.

NOW...

Will you receive the Lord Jesus Christ into your life, as your Lord and Saviour? Will you obey Him, live your life for Him, love Him above all others?

If yes, tell Him, and ask Him to come into your life and into your body to dwell in you, to help you be what He wants you to be. Receive Him, take Him as your own.

IF YOU HAVE THE SON, YOU HAVE LIFE. IF YOU DO NOT HAVE THE SON, YOU DO NOT HAVE LIFE.

'COME TO MY HEART LORD JESUS, THERE IS ROOM IN MY HEART FOR THEE.'

A Prayer of Salvation

Dear Lord,

I admit that I am a sinner and have done many things that don't please you. I have lived my life for myself only. I am sorry, and I repent. I ask you to forgive me.

I believe that you died on the cross for me, to save me. You did what I could not do for myself. I come to you now and ask you to take control of my life; I give it to you. From this day forward, help me to live every day for you, and in a way that pleases you.

I love you, Lord, and I thank you that I will spend all eternity with you. Amen.

(Source: learnreligions.com)

To God be the Glory.

Printed in Great Britain
by Amazon